International Trade Law Statutes and Conventions 2025–2026

International Trade Law Statutes and Conventions 2025–2026 presents all the most recent legislation for international trade law in a student-friendly volume. It can be used alongside *International Trade Law Statutes and Conventions 2019–2021* for a truly comprehensive collection.

Developed in response to feedback from both lecturers and students, the book provides an up-to-date, fully comprehensive collection of current legislation, is curated to align with international trade law courses, is an unannotated text conforming to regulations so that it can be used during exams, features a clear and attractive text design, and includes a detailed table of contents.

Ideal for coursework, exam use, and general reference work, this is the perfect companion for anyone studying this important and fast-moving area of law.

Indira Carr is Professor Emerita at the University of Surrey, UK. She writes extensively on international trade law, corruption, and information technology law. Carr edits *Information and Communications Technology Law* and co-edits *Asian Philosophy*. Both journals are published by Taylor & Francis.

Jae Sundaram is Reader in Trade & Maritime Law at the University of Buckingham, UK. A dual-qualified lawyer, he has published scholarly articles in law of world trade, modern armed-conflict, and is the author of the textbook *WTO Law and Policy: A Political Economy Approach*, and the monograph *Pharmaceutical Patent Protection and World Trade Law*. Both are published by Taylor & Francis (Routledge).

International Trade Law Statutes and Conventions 2025–2026

Indira Carr and Jae Sundaram

Routledge
Taylor & Francis Group
LONDON AND NEW YORK

Designed cover image: Shutterstock

First edition published 2026
by Routledge
4 Park Square, Milton Park, Abingdon, Oxon, OX14 4RN

and by Routledge
605 Third Avenue, New York, NY 10158

Routledge is an imprint of the Taylor & Francis Group, an informa business

British Library Cataloguing-in-Publication Data
A catalogue record for this book is available from the British Library

ISBN: 9781041141679 (hbk)
ISBN: 9781041141686 (pbk)
ISBN: 9781003673194 (ebk)

DOI: 10.4324/ 9781003673194

Typeset in Times New Roman
by Deanta Global Publishing Services, Chennai, India

Contents

Acknowledgements

The publishers and authors thank the following organisations for their permission to reproduce the materials listed:

HCCH (HCCH Principles on Choice of Law in International Commercial Contracts (approved on 19 March 2015))
UNCITRAL (UNCITRAL Model Law on Electronic Transferable Records 2017, UNCITRAL Mediation Rules 2021, UNCITRAL Model Rules on Automated Contracting 2024, UNCITRAL Technical Notes on Online Dispute Resolution 2016).

Preface

The study of International Trade Law requires access to a wide range of materials some of which are not always easily accessible. In 2021, Routledge published *International Trade Law Statutes & Conventions 2019–2021*, edited by us. Since then the legislative landscape has changed since Brexit and is continuously evolving due to greater acceptance of digital technology in trade transactions. This volume reflects some of these changes by including the European Union (Withdrawal) Act 2018, the Private International Law (Implementation of Agreements) Act 2020, and the Retained EU Law (Revocation and Reform) Act 2023, besides the Electronic Trade Documents Act 2023. Model laws drafted by the UNCITRAL, such as their Model Law on Electronic Transferable Records 2017 and Model Rules on Automated Contracting 2024, are also included. This volume is to be treated as a supplement to the collection of statutes and conventions published by Routledge in 2021.

This collection is necessarily highly selective, but we believe that we have included documents that a student is likely to come across in any course on international trade law. This book will also be useful to students following courses on commercial law and carriage of goods. We hope this book will provide a convenient method of access to relevant legislative materials that may not always be easily accessible.

This book is divided into four sections: Statutes; Statutory Instruments; Conventions; and Rules, Model Laws and Technical Notes. The materials in Sections I to III are arranged chronologically and the material in Section IV alphabetically. The material is printed in the amended form, but we have not indicated the source of these amendments and the text is printed as amended even if that amendment is not yet in force. Sections which have been repealed or omitted have been noted.

The collection contains materials available to us up to 1 August 2025.

Indira Carr
Jae Sundaram

Section I

Statutes

1 European Union (Withdrawal) Act 2018

Repeal of the ECA

1 Repeal of the European Communities Act 1972

The European Communities Act 1972 is repealed on exit day.

1A Saving for ECA for implementation period

(1) Subsections (2) to (4) have effect despite the repeal of the European Communities Act 1972 on exit day by section 1.

(2) The European Communities Act 1972, as it has effect in domestic law or the law of a relevant territory immediately before exit day, continues to have effect in domestic law or the law of the relevant territory on and after exit day so far as provided by subsections (3) to (5).

(3) The Act of 1972 has effect on and after exit day as if—

(a) the definitions of "the Treaties" and "the EU Treaties" given by section 1(2) to (4) (interpretation)—

(i) included Part 4 of the withdrawal agreement (implementation period), other than that Part so far as it relates to, or could be applied in relation to, the Common Foreign and Security Policy, but

(ii) were otherwise limited to anything which falls within those definitions as at immediately before exit day so far as it is not excluded by regulations made on or after exit day by a Minister of the Crown under this sub-paragraph,

(b) the reference in section 2(2) to the objects of the EU were a reference to those objects so far as they are applicable to and in the United Kingdom by virtue of Part 4 of the withdrawal agreement,

(c) section 2(3) (payment of EU costs etc.) were omitted,

(d) in section 3 (decisions on, and proof of, EU Treaties and EU instruments etc.)—

DOI: 10.4324/9781003673194-2

(i) the references to the Treaties in subsections (1) and (2) included the withdrawal agreement, and

(ii) the words in brackets in subsection (1) only applied so far as they are in accordance with Part 4 of the withdrawal agreement,

(e) references in sections 5 and 6 (customs duties and common agricultural policy) to the common customs tariff of the EU, directly applicable EU provision, the exclusion of customs duties, EU arrangements and agricultural levies of the EU were to such things so far as they are applicable to and in the United Kingdom by virtue of Part 4 of the withdrawal agreement, and

(f) in Part 2 of Schedule 1 (general definitions in relation to the EU)—

(i) in the definition of "EU customs duty", the reference to directly applicable EU provision were to such provision so far as it is applicable to and in the United Kingdom by virtue of Part 4 of the withdrawal agreement, and

(ii) in the definition of "Member" in the expression "member State", after "EU" there were inserted "and for the purposes of this expression the United Kingdom is to be treated as if it were a member of the EU during the implementation period (within the meaning given by section 1A(6) of the European Union (Withdrawal) Act 2018)".

(4) In this section "relevant territory" means the Isle of Man, any of the Channel Islands or Gibraltar.

(5) Subsections (1) to (4) are repealed on IP completion day.

(6) In this Act—

"the implementation period" means the transition or implementation period provided for by Part 4 of the withdrawal agreement and beginning with exit day and ending on IP completion day;

"IP completion day" (and related expressions) have the same meaning as in the European Union (Withdrawal Agreement) Act 2020 (see section 39(1) to (5) of that Act);

"withdrawal agreement" has the same meaning as in that Act (see section 39(1) and (6) of that Act).

(7) In this Act—

(a) references to the European Communities Act 1972 are to be read, so far as the context permits or requires, as being or (as the case may be) including references to that Act as it continues to have effect by virtue of subsections (2) to (4) above and

(b) references to any Part of the withdrawal agreement or the EEA EFTA separation agreement include references to any other provisions of that agreement so far as applying to that Part.

1B Saving for EU-derived domestic legislation for implementation period

(1) Subsections (2) to (5) have effect despite the repeal of the European Communities Act 1972 on exit day by section 1.

(2) EU-derived domestic legislation, as it has effect in domestic law immediately before exit day, continues to have effect in domestic law on and after exit day, subject as follows.

(3) Any enactment which continues to have effect by virtue of subsection (2) is to be read, on and after exit day and so far as the context permits or requires, as if—

(a) any reference to an expression which is to be read in accordance with Schedule 1 to the Interpretation Act 1978 and is an expression defined by section 1 of, or Part 2 of Schedule 1 to, the European Communities Act 1972 were a reference to that expression as defined by that section or that Part of that Schedule as it continues to have effect by virtue of section 1A(2) to (4) of this Act,

(b) any reference (however expressed and subject to paragraph (a) above) to—

(i) EU law,
(ii) any particular EU Treaty or any part of it,
(iii) any EU instrument, or other document of an EU entity or of the EU, or any part of any such instrument or document,
(iv) any part of EU law not falling within sub-paragraph (ii) or (iii),
(v) any tax, duty, levy or interests of the EU, or
(vi) any arrangement involving, or otherwise relating to, the EU of a kind not falling within sub-paragraph (i), (ii), (iii), (iv) or (v),

were a reference to any such thing so far as it is applicable to and in the United Kingdom by virtue of Part 4 of the withdrawal agreement,

(c) any reference (however expressed and subject to paragraph (a) above) to the European Communities Act 1972 were or (as the case may be) included a reference to the Act of 1972 as it continues to have effect by virtue of section 1A(2) to (4) of this Act,

(d) any reference (however expressed) to the area of the EU or of the EEA included the United Kingdom,

(e) any reference (however expressed) to a citizen of the EU or a national of the EEA included a United Kingdom national (within the meaning given by Article 2(d) of the withdrawal agreement), and

(f) such other modifications were made as—

(i) are provided for by regulations under section 8A or Part 1A of Schedule 2, or

(ii) so far as not so provided, are necessary for any purpose of Part 4 of the withdrawal agreement and are capable of being ascertained from any such purpose or otherwise from that Part of that agreement.

(4) Any EU-derived domestic legislation which is an enactment passed or made on or after exit day and before IP completion day is, unless the contrary intention appears, to be read in accordance with subsection (3) (and anything done or omitted to be done in connection with any such enactment is to be understood, and has effect, accordingly).

(5) Subsections (2) to (4) are subject to any regulations made under section 8A or 23 or Part 1A of Schedule 2 or otherwise under this Act or under the European Union (Withdrawal Agreement) Act 2020.

(6) Subsections (1) to (5) are repealed on IP completion day.

(7) In this Act "EU-derived domestic legislation" means any enactment so far as—

(a) made under section 2(2) of, or paragraph 1A of Schedule 2 to, the European Communities Act 1972,

(b) passed or made, or operating, for a purpose mentioned in section 2(2)(a) or (b) of that Act,

(c) relating to—

(i) anything which falls within paragraph (a) or (b), or

(ii) any rights, powers, liabilities, obligations, restrictions, remedies or procedures which are recognised and available in domestic law by virtue of section 2(1) of the European Communities Act 1972, or

(d) relating otherwise to the EU or the EEA,

but does not include any enactment contained in the European Communities Act 1972 or any enactment contained in this Act or the European Union (Withdrawal Agreement) Act 2020 or in regulations made under this Act or the Act of 2020.

Retention of existing EU law

2 *Saving for EU-derived domestic legislation*

(1) EU-derived domestic legislation, as it has effect in domestic law immediately before IP completion day, continues to have effect in domestic law on and after IP completion day.

(2) … [S. 2(2) omitted]

(3) This section is subject to section 5 and Schedule 1 (exceptions to savings and incorporation) and section 5A (savings and incorporations: supplementary).

3 Incorporation of direct EU legislation

(1) Direct EU legislation, so far as operative immediately before IP completion day, forms part of domestic law on and after IP completion day.
(2) In this Act "direct EU legislation" means—

(a) any EU regulation, EU decision or EU tertiary legislation, as it has effect in EU law immediately before IP completion day and so far as—

(ai) it is applicable to and in the United Kingdom by virtue of Part 4 of the withdrawal agreement,
(bi) it neither has effect nor is to have effect by virtue of section 7A or 7B.

(i) it is not an exempt EU instrument (for which see section 20(1) and Schedule 6), and

(ii) … [S. 3(2)(a)(ii) and word omitted]
(iii) its effect is not reproduced in an enactment to which section 2(1) applies,

(b) any Annex to the EEA agreement, as it has effect in EU law immediately before IP completion day and so far as—

(ai) it is applicable to and in the United Kingdom by virtue of Part 4 of the withdrawal agreement,
(bi) it neither has effect nor is to have effect by virtue of section 7A or 7B.

(i) it refers to, or contains adaptations of, anything falling within paragraph (a), and
(ii) its effect is not reproduced in an enactment to which section 2(1) applies, or

(c) Protocol 1 to the EEA agreement (which contains horizontal adaptations that apply in relation to EU instruments referred to in the Annexes to that agreement), as it has effect in EU law immediately before IP completion day and so far as—

(i) it is applicable to and in the United Kingdom by virtue of Part 4 of the withdrawal agreement, and
(ii) it neither has effect nor is to have effect by virtue of section 7A or 7B.

(3) For the purposes of this Act, any direct EU legislation is operative immediately before IP completion day if—

(a) in the case of anything which comes into force at a particular time and is stated to apply from a later time, it is in force and applies immediately before IP completion day,
(b) in the case of a decision which specifies to whom it is addressed, it has been notified to that person before IP completion day, and
(c) in any other case, it is in force immediately before IP completion day.

(4) This section—

(a) brings into domestic law any direct EU legislation only in the form of the English language version of that legislation, and
(b) does not apply to any such legislation for which there is no such version,

but paragraph (a) does not affect the use of the other language versions of that legislation for the purposes of interpreting it.

(5) This section is subject to section 5 and Schedule 1 (exceptions to savings and incorporation) and section 5A (savings and incorporation: supplementary).

4 Saving for rights etc. under section 2(1) of the ECA

(1) … [S. 4 repealed]

5 Exceptions to savings and incorporation

(A1) The principle of the supremacy of EU law is not part of domestic law. This applies after the end of 2023, in relation to any enactment or rule of law (whether pass or made)

(A2) Any provision of assimilated direct legislation—

(a) must, so far as possible, be read and given effect in a way which is compatible with all domestic enactments, and
(b) is subject to all domestic enactment, so far as it is incompatible with them.

(A3) Subsection (A2) is subject to—

(a) section 186 of the Data Protection Act 2018 (data subject's rights and other prohibitions and restrictions)
(b) regulations under section 7(1) of the Retained EU Law (Revocation and Reform) Act 2023.

(A4) No general principle of EU law is part of domestic law after the end of 2023.

(1)—(3) … [S. 5(1)—(3) omitted]

(4) The Charter of Fundamental Rights is not part of domestic law on or after IP completion day.
(5) … [S. 5(5) omitted]
(6) Schedule 1 (which makes further provision about exceptions to savings and incorporation) has effect.
(7) Subsection (A1) to (6) and Schedule 1 are subject to relevant separation agreement law (for which see section 7C).
(8) In this section "domestic enactment" means an enactment other than one consisting of assimilated direct legislation.

5A Savings and incorporation: supplementary

The fact that anything which continues to be, or forms part of, domestic law on or after IP completion day by virtue of section 2 or 3 has an effect immediately before IP completion day which is time-limited by reference to the implementation period does not prevent it from having an indefinite effect on and after IP completion day by virtue of section 2 or 3.

6 Interpretation of assimilated law

(1) A court or tribunal—

 (a) is not bound by any principles laid down, or any decisions made, on or after IP completion day by the European Court, and
 (b) cannot refer any matter to the European Court on or after IP completion day.

(2) Subject to this and subsections (3) to (6), a court or tribunal may have regard to anything done on or after IP completion day by the European Court, another EU entity or the EU so far as it is relevant to any matter before the court or tribunal.
(3) Any question as to the validity, meaning or effect of any assimilated law is to be decided, so far as that law is unmodified on or after IP completion day and so far as they are relevant to it—

 (a) in accordance with any assimilated EU case law and any retained general principles of EU law, and
 (b) having regard (among other things) to the limits, immediately before IP completion day, of EU competences.

(4) But—

(a) the Supreme Court is not bound by any assimilated EU case law,
(b) the High Court of Justiciary is not bound by any assimilated EU case law when—

(i) sitting as a court of appeal otherwise than in relation to a compatibility issue (within the meaning given by section 288ZA(2) of the Criminal Procedure (Scotland) Act 1995) or a devolution issue (within the meaning given by paragraph 1 of Schedule 6 to the Scotland Act 1998), or
(ii) sitting on a reference under section 123(1) of the Criminal Procedure (Scotland) Act 1995, and

(ba) a relevant court or relevant tribunal is not bound by any assimilated EU case law so far as is provided for by regulations under subsection (5A), and
(c) no court or tribunal is bound by any assimilated domestic case law that it would not otherwise be bound by.

(5) In deciding whether to depart from any assimilated EU case law by virtue of subsection (4)(a) or (b), the Supreme Court or the High Court of Justiciary must apply the same test as it would apply in deciding whether to depart from its own case law.

(5A) A minister of the Crown may by regulations provide for—

(a) a court or tribunal to be a relevant court or (as the case may be) a relevant tribunal for the purposes of this section,
(b) the extent to which, or circumstances in which, a relevant court or relevant tribunal is not to be bound by retained EU case law,
(c) the test which a relevant court or relevant tribunal must apply in deciding whether to depart from any retained EU case law, or
(d) considerations which are to be relevant to—

(i) the Supreme Court or the High Court of Justiciary in applying the test mentioned in subsection (5), or
(ii) a relevant court or relevant tribunal in applying any test provided for by virtue of paragraph (c) above.

(5B) Regulations under subsection (5A) may (among other things) provide for—

(a) the High Court of Justiciary to be a relevant court when sitting otherwise than as mentioned in subsection (4)(b)(i) and (ii)
(b) the extent to which, or circumstances in which, a relevant court or relevant tribunal not being bound by retained EU case law includes (or does not include) that court or tribunal not being bound by retained domestic case law which relates to retained EU case law,

(c) other matters arising in relation to retained domestic case law which relates to retained EU case law (including by making provision of a kind which could be made in relation to retained EU case law), or

(d) the test mentioned in paragraph (c) of subsection (5A) or the considerations mentioned in paragraph (d) of that subsection to be determined (whether with or without the consent of a Minister of the Crown) by a person mentioned in subsection (5C)(a) to

(e) or by more than one of those persons acting jointly.

(5C) Before making regulations under subsection (5A), a Minister of the Crown must consult—

(a) the President of the Supreme Court,
(b) the Lord Chief Justice of England and Wales,
(c) the Lord President of the Court of Session,
(d) the Lord Chief Justice of Northern Ireland,
(e) the Senior President of Tribunals, and
(f) such other persons as the Minister of the Crown considers appropriate.

(5D) No regulations may be made under subsection (5A) after IP completion day.

(6) Subsection (3) does not prevent the validity, meaning or effect of any assimilated law which has been modified on or after IP implementation day from being decided as provided for in that subsection if doing so is consistent with the intention of the modifications.

(6A) Subsections (1) to (6) are subject to relevant separation agreement law (for which see section 7C)

(7) In this Act—

"assimilated case law" means—

(a) assimilated domestic case law, and
(b) assimilated EU case law;

"assimilated domestic case law" means any principles laid down by, and any decisions of, a court or tribunal in the United Kingdom, as they have effect immediately before exit day and so far as they—

(a) relate to anything to which section 2, 3 or 4 applies, and
(b) are not excluded by section 5 or Schedule 1,

(as those principles and decisions are modified by or under this Act or by other domestic law from time to time);

"assimilated EU case law" means any principles laid down by, and any decisions of, the European Court, as they have effect in EU law immediately before exit day and so far as they—

(a) relate to anything to which section 2, 3 or 4 applies, and
(b) are not excluded by section 5 or Schedule 1,

(as those principles and decisions are modified by or under this Act or by other domestic law from time to time);

"assimilated EU law" means anything which, on or after IP completion day, continues to be, or forms part of, domestic law by virtue of section 2 or 3 or subsection (3) or (6) above (as that body of law is added to or otherwise modified by or under this Act or by other domestic law from time to time);

[Words in S. 6(7) omitted]

[Words in S. 6(7) omitted]

6D Incompatibility orders

(1) This section applies if a court or tribunal decides, in the course of any proceedings—

(a) that a provision of assimilated direct legislation is incompatible with, and by virtue of section 5(A2)(b) subject to, any domestic enactment, or
(b) that a domestic enactment is incompatible with, and by virtue of section 7(1) of the Retained EU Law (Revocation and Reform) Act 2023 subject to, a provision of assimilated direct legislation.

(2) The court or tribunal must make an order (an "incompatibility order") to that effect (in addition to any exercise of other powers that it may have in relation to the proceedings).
(3) An incompatibility order may (among other things)—

(a) set out the effect of the relevant provision in its operation in relation to that particular case;
(b) delay the coming into force of the order;
(c) remove or limit any effect of the operation of the relevant provision before the coming into force of the order.

(4) Provision included in an incompatibility order may be made subject to conditions.
(5) In this section—

"domestic enactment" has the same meaning as in section 5 of this Act;

"the relevant provision" means section 5(A2)(b) of this Act or section 7(1) of the Retained EU Law (Revocation and Reform) Act 2023 (as the case may be).

7 *Status of retained EU law*

(1) Anything which—

(a) was, immediately before exit day, primary legislation of a particular kind, subordinate legislation of a particular kind or another enactment of a particular kind, and
(b) continues to be domestic law on and after exit day by virtue of section 1A(2) or 1B(2),

continues to be domestic law as an enactment of the same kind.

(1A) Anything which—

(a) was, immediately before IP completion day, primary legislation of a particular kind, subordinate legislation of a particular kind or another enactment of a particular kind, and
(b) continues to be domestic law on and after IP completion day by virtue of section 2,

continues to be domestic law as an enactment of the same kind.

(4A) Assimilated direct legislation may only be modified by—

- primary legislation, or
- subordinate legislation so far as it is made under a power which permits such a modification by virtue of—

  (i) paragraph 3, 8(3), 11A, 11B or 12(3) of Schedule 8
  (ii) any other provision made by or under this Act,
  (iii) any provision made by or under an Act of Parliament passed before, and in the same Session as, this Act, or
  (iv) any provision made on or after the passing of this Act by or under primary legislation.

(5) For other provisions about the status of retained EU law, see—

(a) section 5 (A1) to (A3) and (7) (status of assimilated law in relation to other enactments or rules of law),
(b) section 6 (status of assimilated case law … [Words in s. 7(5)(b) omitted],
(ba) section 7C (status of case law of European Court etc. in relation to assimilated law which is relevant separation agreement law),
(c) section 15(2) and Part 2 of Schedule 5 (status of assimilated law for the purposes of the rules of evidence),
(d) paragraph 16 of Schedule 8 (information about Scottish instruments which amend or revoke subordinate legislation under section 2(2) of the European Communities Act 1972),

(e) paragraphs 19 and 20 of that Schedule (status of certain assimilated direct legislation for the purposes of the Interpretation Act 1978), and

(f) paragraph 30 of that Schedule (status of assimilated direct legislation for the purposes of the Human Rights Act 1998).

(6) … [S. 7(6) omitted]

7A General implementation of reminder of withdrawal agreement

(1) Subsection (2) applies to—

(a) all such rights, powers, liabilities, obligations and restrictions from time to time created or arising by or under the withdrawal agreement, and

(b) all such remedies and procedures from time to time provided for by or under the withdrawal agreement,

as in accordance with the withdrawal agreement are without further enactment to be given legal effect or used in the United Kingdom.

(2) The rights, powers, liabilities, obligations, restrictions, remedies and procedures concerned are to be—

(a) recognised and available in domestic law, and

(b) enforced, allowed and followed accordingly.

(3) Every enactment (including an enactment contained in this Act) is to be read and has effect subject to subsection (2).

(3A) The following provide for the application in Northern Ireland of EU law relating to the trade in goods necessary for the functioning of the Windsor Framework in the withdrawal agreement to be subject to democratic consent and scrutiny—

(a) Articles 13 and 18 of that Framework, and

(b) Part 5A of the Northern Ireland Act 1998.

(4) This section does not apply in relation to Part 4 of the withdrawal agreement so far as section 2(1) of the European Communities Act 1972 applies in relation to that Part.

(5) See also (among other things)—

(a) Part 3 of the European Union (Withdrawal Agreement) Act 2020 (further provision about citizens' rights),

(b) section 20 of that Act (financial provision),

(c) section 7C of this Act (interpretation of law relating to withdrawal agreement etc.),

(d) section 8B of this Act (power in connection with certain other separation issues),
(e) section 8C of this Act (power in connection with the Protocol on Ireland/Northern Ireland in withdrawal agreement), and
(f) Parts 1B and 1C of Schedule 2 to this Act (powers involving devolved authorities in connection with certain other separation issues and the Ireland/Northern Ireland Protocol).

7B General implementation of EEA EFTA and Swiss agreements

7 B & 7C [Omitted]

8 Dealing with deficiencies arising from withdrawal

(1) A Minister of the Crown may by regulations make such provision as the Minister considers appropriate to prevent, remedy or mitigate—

(a) any failure of retained EU law to operate effectively, or
(b) any other deficiency in retained EU law,

arising from the withdrawal of the United Kingdom from the EU.

(2) Deficiencies in retained EU law are where the Minister considers that retained EU law—

(a) contains anything which has no practical application in relation to the United Kingdom or any part of it or is otherwise redundant or substantially redundant,
(b) confers functions on, or in relation to, EU entities which no longer have functions in that respect under EU law in relation to the United Kingdom or any part of it,
(c) makes provision for, or in connection with, reciprocal arrangements between—

(i) the United Kingdom or any part of it or a public authority in the United Kingdom, and
(ii) the EU, an EU entity, a member State or a public authority in a member State,

which no longer exist or are no longer appropriate,

(d) makes provision for, or in connection with, other arrangements which—

(i) involve the EU, an EU entity, a member State or a public authority in a member State, or

(ii) are otherwise dependent upon the United Kingdom's membership of the EU or Part 4 of the withdrawal agreement,

and which no longer exist or are no longer appropriate,

(e) makes provision for, or in connection with, any reciprocal or other arrangements not falling within paragraph (c) or (d) which no longer exist, or are no longer appropriate, as a result of the United Kingdom ceasing to be a party to any of the EU Treaties or as a result of either the end of the implementation period or any other effect of the withdrawal agreement,

(ee) is not clear in its effect as a result of the operation of any provision of sections 2 to 6 or Schedule 1

(f) does not contain any functions or restrictions which—

(i) were in an EU directive and in force immediately before IP completion day (including any power to make EU tertiary legislation), and

(ii) it is appropriate to retain, or

(g) contains EU references which are no longer appropriate.

(3) There is also a deficiency in retained EU law where the Minister considers that there is—

(a) anything in retained EU law which is of a similar kind to any deficiency which falls within subsection (2), or

(b) a deficiency in retained EU law of a kind described, or provided for, in regulations made by a Minister of the Crown.

(4) But retained EU law is not deficient merely because it does not contain any modification of EU law which is adopted or notified, comes into force or only applies on or after IP completion day.

(5) Regulations under subsection (1) may make any provision that could be made by an Act of Parliament.

(6) Regulations under subsection (1) may (among other things) provide for functions of EU entities or public authorities in member States (including making an instrument of a legislative character or providing funding) to be—

(a) exercisable instead by a public authority (whether or not established for the purpose) in the United Kingdom, or

(b) replaced, abolished or otherwise modified.

(7) But regulations under subsection (1) may not—

(a) impose or increase taxation or fees,

(b) make retrospective provision,

(c) create a relevant criminal offence,
(d) establish a public authority,
(e) … [S. 8(7) omitted]
(f) amend, repeal or revoke the Human Rights Act 1998 or any subordinate legislation made under it, or
(g) amend or repeal the Scotland Act 1998, the Government of Wales Act 2006 or the Northern Ireland Act 1998 (unless the regulations are made by virtue of paragraph 21(b) of Schedule 7 to this Act or are amending or repealing any provision of those Acts which modifies another enactment).

(8) No regulations may be made under this section after the end of the period of two years beginning with IP completion day.

(9) The reference in subsection (1) to a failure or other deficiency arising from the withdrawal of the United Kingdom from the EU includes a reference to any failure or other deficiency arising from

(a) any aspect of the withdrawal, including (among other things)—

(i) the end of the implementation period, or
(ii) any other effect of the withdrawal agreement, or

(b) that withdrawal, or any such aspect of it, taken together with the operation of any provision, or the interaction between any provisions, made by or under this Act or the European Union (Withdrawal Agreement) Act 2020.

8A Supplementary power in connection with implementation period

(1) A Minister of the Crown may by regulations—

(a) provide for other modifications for the purposes of section 1B(3)(f)(i) (whether applying in all cases or particular cases or descriptions of case),
(b) provide for subsection (3) or (4) of section 1B not to apply to any extent in particular cases or descriptions of case,
(c) make different provision in particular cases or descriptions of case to that made by subsection (3) or (4) of that section,
(d) modify any enactment contained in this Act in consequence of any repeal made by section 1A(5) or 1B(6), or
(e) make such provision not falling within paragraph (a), (b), (c) or (d) as the Minister considers appropriate for any purpose of, or otherwise in connection with, Part 4 of the withdrawal agreement.

(2) The power to make regulations under subsection (1) may (among other things) be exercised by modifying any provision made by or under an enactment.

(3) In subsection (2) "enactment" does not include primary legislation passed or made after IP completion day.

(4) No regulations may be made under subsection (1) after the end of the period of two years beginning with IP completion day.

8B Power in connection with certain other separation issues

(1) A Minister of the Crown may by regulations make such provision as the Minister considers appropriate—

  (a) to implement Part 3 of the withdrawal agreement (separation provisions),
  (b) to supplement the effect of section 7A in relation to that Part, or
  (c) otherwise for the purposes of dealing with matters arising out of, or related to, that Part (including matters arising by virtue of section 7A and that Part).

(2) A Minister of the Crown may by regulations make such provision as the Minister considers appropriate—

  (a) to implement Part 3 of the EEA EFTA separation agreement (separation provisions),
  (b) to supplement the effect of section 7B in relation to that Part, or
  (c) otherwise for the purposes of dealing with matters arising out of, or related to, that Part (including matters arising by virtue of section 7B and that Part).

(3) Regulations under this section may make any provision that could be made by an Act of Parliament.

(4) Regulations under this section may (among other things) restate, for the purposes of making the law clearer or more accessible, anything that forms part of domestic law by virtue of—

  (a) section 7A above and Part 3 of the withdrawal agreement, or
  (b) section 7B above and Part 3 of the EEA EFTA separation agreement.

(5) But regulations under this section may not—

  (a) impose or increase taxation or fees,
  (b) make retrospective provision,
  (c) create a relevant criminal offence,
  (d) establish a public authority,
  (e) amend, repeal or revoke the Human Rights Act 1998 or any subordinate legislation made under it, or
  (f) amend or repeal the Scotland Act 1998, the Government of Wales Act 2006 or the Northern Ireland Act 1998 (unless the regulations

are made by virtue of paragraph 21(b) of Schedule 7 to this Act or are amending or repealing any provision of those Acts which modifies another enactment).

(6) In this section references to Part 3 of the withdrawal agreement or of the EEA EFTA separation agreement include references to any provision of EU law which is applied by, or referred to in, that Part (to the extent of the application or reference).

8C Power in connection with Ireland/Northern Ireland Protocol in withdrawal agreement

(1) A Minister of the Crown may by regulations make such provision as the Minister considers appropriate—

(a) to implement the Protocol on Ireland/Northern Ireland in the withdrawal agreement,
(b) to supplement the effect of section 7A in relation to the Protocol, or
(c) otherwise for the purposes of dealing with matters arising out of, or related to, the Protocol (including matters arising by virtue of section 7A and the Protocol).

(2) Regulations under subsection (1) may make any provision that could be made by an Act of Parliament (including modifying this Act).
(3) Regulations under subsection (1) may (among other things) make provision facilitating the access to the market within Great Britain of qualifying Northern Ireland goods.
(4) Such provision may (among other things) include provision about the recognition within Great Britain of technical regulations, assessments, registrations, certificates, approvals and authorisations issued by—

(a) the authorities of a member State, or
(b) bodies established in a member State, in respect of qualifying Northern Ireland goods.

(5) Regulations under subsection (1) may (among other things) restate, for the purposes of making the law clearer or more accessible, anything that forms part of domestic law by virtue of section 7A and the Protocol.

(5A) Regulations under subsection (1) may not amend, repeal or otherwise modify the operation of section 47 of the United Kingdom Internal Market Act 2020 ("the 2020 Act"), except by making—

(a) provision of the sort that is contemplated by section 47(2) of the 2020 Act (permitted checks);
(b) provision under subsection (6);

(c) provision of the sort described in paragraph 21(b) of Schedule 7 (supplementary and transitional provision etc) in connection with—

(i) provision within either of the preceding paragraphs;
(ii) Articles 5 to 10 of the Northern Ireland Protocol ceasing to apply (and the resulting operation of section 55(1) of the 2020 Act).

(6) A Minister of the Crown may by regulations define "qualifying Northern Ireland goods" for the purposes of this Act.
(7) In this section any reference to the Protocol on Ireland/Northern Ireland includes a reference to—

(a) any other provision of the withdrawal agreement so far as applying to the Protocol, and
(b) any provision of EU law which is applied by, or referred to in, the Protocol (to the extent of the application or reference),

but does not include the second sentence of Article 11(1) of the Protocol (which provides that the United Kingdom and the Republic of Ireland may continue to make new arrangements that build on the provisions of the Belfast Agreement in other areas of North-South cooperation on the island of Ireland).

9 Implementing the withdrawal agreement

[S. 9 repealed]

Devolution

10 Protection for North-South co-operation and the prevention of new border arrangements

(1) In exercising any of the powers under this Act, a Minister of the Crown or devolved authority must—

(a) act in a way that is compatible with the terms of the Northern Ireland Act 1998, and
(b) have due regard to the joint report from the negotiators of the EU and the United Kingdom Government on progress during phase 1 of negotiations under Article 50 of the Treaty on European Union.

(2) Nothing in section 8, or 23(1) or (6) of this Act authorises regulations which—

(a) diminish any form of North-South cooperation provided for by the Belfast Agreement (as defined by section 98 of the Northern Ireland Act 1998), or
(b) create or facilitate border arrangements between Northern Ireland and the Republic of Ireland after exit day which feature physical infrastructure, including border posts, or checks and controls, that did not exist before exit day and are not in accordance with an agreement between the United Kingdom and the EU.

(3) A Minister of the Crown may not agree to the making of a recommendation by the Joint Committee under Article 11(2) of the Protocol on Ireland/Northern Ireland in the withdrawal agreement (recommendations as to North-South cooperation) to—

(a) alter the arrangements for North-South co-operation as provided for by the Belfast Agreement,
(b) establish a new implementation body, or
(c) alter the functions of an existing implementation body.

(4) In this section—

"the Belfast Agreement" has the meaning given by section 98 of the Northern Ireland Act 1998;
"implementation body" has the meaning given by section 55(3) of that Act.

11 Powers involving devolved authorities corresponding to sections 8 to 8C

Schedule 2 (which confers powers to make regulations involving devolved authorities which correspond to the powers conferred by sections 8 to 8C) has effect.

12 Retaining EU restrictions in devolution legislation etc.

[Omitted]

13 Parliamentary approval of the outcome of negotiations with the EU

[S. 13 repealed]

13A Review of EU Legislation during implementation period

[Omitted]

13B Certain dispute procedure under withdrawal agreement

(1) Subsection (2) if a request has been made under Article 170 of the withdrawal agreement to the other party in a dispute (request to establish an arbitration panel in relation to a dispute between the EU and the United Kingdom).

(2) A Minister of the Crown must, within the 14 day period beginning with the day on which the request is made, make a statement in writing to each House of Parliament that the request has been made and setting out the details of it.

(3) Subsection (4) applies if the European Court has given a ruling in response to a request by an arbitration panel under Article 174(1) of the withdrawal agreement (request for ruling by European Court on certain questions arising in a dispute submitted to arbitration).

(4) A Minister of the Crown must, within the 14 day period beginning with the publication in the Official Journal of the European Union of the ruling of the European Court, make a statement in writing to each House of Parliament that the ruling has been made and setting out the details of it contained in the Official Journal.

(5) After the end of each reporting period, a Minister of the Crown must lay before each House of Parliament a report setting out the number of times within the reporting period that the Joint Committee has been provided with notice under Article 169(1) of the withdrawal agreement (notice concerning the commencement of consultations in the Joint Committee to resolve a dispute between the EU and the United Kingdom about the interpretation and application of the withdrawal agreement).

(6) In this section—

"reporting period" means—

(a) the period of one year beginning with the day on which IP completion day falls, and

(b) each subsequent year;

"the 14 day period" means—

(a) in relation to the House of Commons, the period of 14 Commons sitting days, and

(b) in relation to the House of Lords, the period of 14 Lords sitting days.

13C Bills affecting trade between Northern Ireland and other parts of the United Kingdom

(1) This section applies where a Minister of the Crown in charge of a Bill in either House of Parliament is of the view that the Bill as introduced

into that House contains provision which, if enacted, would affect trade between Northern Ireland and other parts of the United Kingdom.

(2) The Minister in charge of the Bill must, before Second Reading of the Bill in the House in question, make—

(a) a statement to the effect that in the Minister's view the Bill does not contain provision which, if enacted, would have a significant adverse effect on trade between Northern Ireland and the rest of the United Kingdom, or

(b) a statement to the effect that the Minister is unable to make such a statement but His Majesty's Government nevertheless wishes the House to proceed with the Bill.

(3) A statement under this section must be in writing and be published in such manner as the Minister considers appropriate.

14 Financial provision

(1) Schedule 4 (which contains powers in connection with fees and charges) has effect.

(2) A Minister of the Crown, government department or devolved authority may incur expenditure, for the purpose of, or in connection with, preparing for anything about which provision may be made under a power to make subordinate legislation conferred or modified by or under this Act, before any such provision is made.

(3) There is to be paid out of money provided by Parliament—

(a) any expenditure incurred by a Minister of the Crown, government department or other public authority by virtue of this Act, and

(b) any increase attributable to this Act in the sums payable by virtue of any other Act out of money so provided.

(4) Subsection (3) is subject to any other provision made by or under this Act or any other enactment.

15 Publication and rules of evidence

[Omitted]

15A Prohibition on extending implementation period

A Minister of the Crown may not agree in the Joint Committee to an extension of the implementation period.

15B Ministerial co-chairs of the Joint Committee

The functions of the United Kingdom's co-chair of the Joint Committee, under Annex VIII of the withdrawal agreement (rules of procedure of the Joint Committee and specialised committees), are to be exercised personally by a Minister of the Crown (and, accordingly, only a Minister of the Crown may be designated as a replacement under Rule 1(3)).

15C No use of written procedure in the Joint Committee

(1) The United Kingdom's co-chair of the Joint Committee may not consent to the Joint Committee using the written procedure provided for in Rule 9(1) of Annex VIII of the withdrawal agreement.
(2) In subsection (1) the reference to the United Kingdom's co-chair of the Joint Committee includes a reference to any designee of the co-chair designated under Rule 1(3) of Annex VIII of the withdrawal agreement.

16 Maintenance of environmental principles etc.

[S. 16 repealed]

17 Family unity for those seeking asylum or other protection in Europe

[Omitted]

18 Customs arrangement as part of the framework for the future relationship

[S. 18 repealed]

19 Future interaction with the law and agencies of the EU

[S. 19 repealed]

General and final provision

20 Interpretation

(1) In this Act—

"assimilated direct legislation" means any direct EU legislation which forms part of domestic law by virtue of section 3 (as modified by or under this Act or by other domestic law from time to time, and including any instruments made under it on or after IP completion day);

"assimilated direct minor legislation" means any assimilated direct legislation which is not assimilated direct principal legislation;

"assimilated direct principal legislation" means—

(a) any EU regulation so far as it—

(i) forms part of domestic law on and after IP completion day by virtue of section 3, and

(ii) was not EU tertiary legislation immediately before IP completion day, or

(b) any Annex to the EEA agreement so far as it—

(i) forms part of domestic law on and after IP completion day by virtue of section 3, and

(ii) refers to, or contains adaptations of, any EU regulation so far as it falls within paragraph (a),

(as modified by or under this Act or by other domestic law from time to time);

"Charter of Fundamental Rights" means the Charter of Fundamental Rights of the European Union of 7 December 2000, as adapted at Strasbourg on 12 December 2007;

"Commons sitting day" means a day on which the House of Commons is sitting (and a day is only a day on which the House of Commons is sitting if the House begins to sit on that day);

"devolved authority" means—

(a) the Scottish Ministers,

(b) the Welsh Ministers, or

(c) a Northern Ireland department;

"domestic law" means—

(a) in section 3, 7A and 7B, the law of England and Wales, Scotland and Northern Ireland, and

(b) in any other case, the law of England and Wales, Scotland or Northern Ireland;

"the EEA" means the European Economic Area;

"enactment" means an enactment whenever passed or made and includes—

(a) an enactment contained in any Order in Council, order, rules, regulations, scheme, warrant, byelaw or other instrument made under an Act,

(b) an enactment contained in any Order in Council made in exercise of Her Majesty's Prerogative,
(c) an enactment contained in, or in an instrument made under, an Act of the Scottish Parliament,
(d) an enactment contained in, or in an instrument made under, a Measure or Act of the National Assembly for Wales,
(e) an enactment contained in, or in an instrument made under, Northern Ireland legislation,
(f) an enactment contained in any instrument made by a member of the Scottish Government, the Welsh Ministers, the First Minister for Wales, the Counsel General to the Welsh Government, a Northern Ireland Minister, the First Minister in Northern Ireland, the deputy First Minister in Northern Ireland or a Northern Ireland department in exercise of prerogative or other executive functions of Her Majesty which are exercisable by such a person on behalf of Her Majesty,
(g) an enactment contained in, or in an instrument made under, a Measure of the Church Assembly or of the General Synod of the Church of England, and
(h) except in sections 1B and 7 or where there is otherwise a contrary intention, any assimilated direct legislation;

"EU decision" means—

(a) a decision within the meaning of Article 288 of the Treaty on the Functioning of the European Union, or
(b) a decision under former Article 34(2)(c) of the Treaty on European Union;

"EU directive" means a directive within the meaning of Article 288 of the Treaty on the Functioning of the European Union;
"EU entity" means an EU institution or any office, body or agency of the EU;
"EU reference" means—

(a) any reference to the EU, an EU entity or a member State,
(b) any reference to an EU directive or any other EU law, or
(c) any other reference which relates to the EU;

"EU regulation" means a regulation within the meaning of Article 288 of the Treaty on the Functioning of the European Union;
"EU tertiary legislation" means—

(a) any provision made under—

(i) an EU regulation,
(ii) a decision within the meaning of Article 288 of the Treaty on the Functioning of the European Union, or
(iii) an EU directive,

by virtue of Article 290 or 291(2) of the Treaty on the Functioning of the European Union or former Article 202 of the Treaty establishing the European Community, or

(b) any measure adopted in accordance with former Article 34(2)(c) of the Treaty on European Union to implement decisions under former Article 34(2)(c),

but does not include any such provision or measure which is an EU directive;

"exempt EU instrument" means anything which is an exempt EU instrument by virtue of Schedule 6;

"exit day" means 31 January 2020 at 11.00 p.m. (and see subsections (2) to (5));

"future relationship agreement" has the same meaning as in the European Union (Future Relationship) Act 2020 (see section 37 of that Act);

"Joint Committee" means the Joint Committee established by Article 164(1) of the withdrawal agreement;

"Lords sitting day" means a day on which the House of Lords is sitting (and a day is only a day on which the House of Lords is sitting if the House begins to sit on that day);

"member State" (except in the definitions of "direct EU legislation" and "EU reference") does not include the United Kingdom;

"Minister of the Crown" has the same meaning as in the Ministers of the Crown Act 1975 and also includes the Commissioners for Her Majesty's Revenue and Customs;

"modify" includes amend, repeal or revoke (and related expressions are to be read accordingly);

"Northern Ireland devolved authority" means the First Minister and deputy First Minister in Northern Ireland acting jointly, a Northern Ireland Minister or a Northern Ireland department;

"primary legislation" means—

(a) an Act of Parliament,
(b) an Act of the Scottish Parliament,
(c) a Measure or Act of the National Assembly for Wales, or
(d) Northern Ireland legislation;

"public authority" means a public authority within the meaning of section 6 of the Human Rights Act 1998;

"ratify", whether in relation to the withdrawal agreement or otherwise, has the same meaning as it does for the purposes of Part 2 of the Constitutional Reform and Governance Act 2010 in relation to a treaty (see section 25 of that Act);

"relevant criminal offence" means an offence for which an individual who has reached the age of 18 (or, in relation to Scotland or Northern Ireland, 21) is capable of being sentenced to imprisonment for a term of more than 2 years (ignoring any enactment prohibiting or restricting the imprisonment of individuals who have no previous convictions);

"retrospective provision", in relation to provision made by regulations, means provision taking effect from a date earlier than the date on which the regulations are made;

"subordinate legislation" means—

(a) any Order in Council, order, rules, regulations, scheme, warrant, byelaw or other instrument made under any Act, or

(b) any instrument made under an Act of the Scottish Parliament, Northern Ireland legislation or a Measure or Act of the National Assembly for Wales,

and (except in section 7 or Schedule 2 or where there is a contrary intention) includes any Order in Council, order, rules, regulations, scheme, warrant, byelaw or other instrument made on or after IP completion day under any assimilated direct legislation;

"tribunal" means any tribunal in which legal proceedings may be brought;

"Wales" and "Welsh zone" have the same meaning as in the Government of Wales Act 2006 (see section 158 of that Act);

(2) In this Act references to before, after or on exit day, or to beginning with exit day, are to be read as references to before, after or at 11.00 p.m. on 31 January 2020 or (as the case may be) to beginning with 11.00 p.m. on that day.

(3) Subsection (4) applies if the day or time on or at which the Treaties are to cease to apply to the United Kingdom in accordance with Article 50(3) of the Treaty on European Union is different from that specified in the definition of "exit day" in subsection (1).

(4) A Minister of the Crown must by regulations—

(a) amend the definition of "exit day" in subsection (1) to ensure that the day and time specified in the definition are the day and time that the Treaties are to cease to apply to the United Kingdom, and

(b) amend subsection (2) in consequence of any such amendment.

(5) In subsections (3) and (4) "the Treaties" means the Treaty on European Union and the Treaty on the Functioning of the European Union.

(5A) In this Act references to anything which continues to be domestic law by virtue of section 1B(2) include—

(a) references to anything to which section 1B(2) applies which continues to be domestic law on or after exit day (whether or not it would have done so irrespective of that provision), and
(b) references to anything which continues to be domestic law on or after exit day by virtue of section 1B(2) (as that body of law is added to or otherwise modified by or under this Act or by other domestic law from time to time).

(6) In this Act references to anything which continues to be domestic law by virtue of section 2 include references to anything to which subsection (1) of that section applies which continues to be domestic law on or after IP completion day (whether or not it would have done so irrespective of that section).
(7) [omitted]
(8) References in this Act (however expressed) to a public authority in the United Kingdom include references to a public authority in any part of the United Kingdom.
(9) References in this Act to former Article 34(2)(c) of the Treaty on European Union are references to that Article as it had effect at any time before the coming into force of the Treaty of Lisbon.
(10) Any other reference in this Act to—

(a) an Article of the Treaty on European Union or the Treaty on the Functioning of the European Union, or
(b) Article 10 of Title VII of Protocol 36 to those treaties,

includes a reference to that Article as applied by Article 106a of the Euratom Treaty.

21 Index of defined expressions

[Omitted]

22 Regulations

Schedule 7 (which makes provision about the scrutiny by Parliament and the devolved legislatures of regulations under this Act and contains other general provision about such regulations) has effect.

23 Consequential and transitional provision

(1) A Minister of the Crown may by regulations make such provision as the Minister considers appropriate in consequence of this Act.

(2) The power to make regulations under subsection (1) may (among other things) be exercised by modifying any provision made by or under an enactment.

(3) In subsection (2) "enactment" does not include primary legislation passed or made after IP completion day.

(4) No regulations may be made under subsection (1) after the end of the period of 10 years beginning with IP completion day.

(5) Parts 1 and 2 of Schedule 8 (which contain consequential provision) have effect.

(6) A Minister of the Crown may by regulations make such transitional, transitory or saving provision as the Minister considers appropriate in connection with the coming into force of any provision of this Act (including its operation in connection with IP completion day).

(7) Parts 3 and 4 of Schedule 8 (which contain transitional, transitory and saving provision) have effect.

(8) The enactments mentioned in Schedule 9 (which contains repeals not made elsewhere in this Act) are repealed to the extent specified.

24 Extent

(1) Subject to subsections (2) and (3), this Act extends to England and Wales, Scotland and Northern Ireland.

(2) Any provision of this Act which amends or repeals an enactment has the same extent as the enactment amended or repealed.

(3) Regulations under section 8(1) or 23 may make provision which extends to Gibraltar—

(a) modifying any enactment which—

(j) extends to Gibraltar and relates to European Parliamentary elections, or

(iii) extends to Gibraltar for any purpose which is connected with Gibraltar forming part of an electoral region, under the European Parliamentary Elections Act 2002, for the purposes of such elections, or

(b) which is supplementary, incidental, consequential, transitional, transitory or saving provision in connection with a modification within paragraph (a).

25 Commencement and short title

[Omitted]

Schedules 1–8

[Omitted]

2 Private International Law (Implementation of Agreements) Act 2020

Implementation of international agreements

1 Implementation of the 1996, 2005 and 2007 Hague Conventions

(1) In the Civil Jurisdiction and Judgments Act 1982 ("the 1982 Act"), in subsection (1) of section 1 (interpretation of references to the Conventions etc) insert at the appropriate place—

""the 1996 Hague Convention" means the Convention on Jurisdiction, Applicable Law, Recognition, Enforcement and Co-operation in respect of Parental Responsibility and Measures for the Protection of Children concluded on 19th October 1996 at The Hague".

(2) Before section 4 of the 1982 Act (and before the italic heading preceding that section) insert—

"3C The 1996 Hague Convention to have the force of law

(1) The 1996 Hague Convention shall have the force of law in the United Kingdom.
(2) For the purposes of this Act the 1996 Hague Convention is to be read together with the following declarations made by the United Kingdom on 27th July 2012—

(a) the declaration under Article 29 of the Convention, concerning applicable territorial units;
(b) the declaration under Article 34 of the Convention, concerning communication of requests under paragraph 1 of that Article;
(c) the declaration under Article 54 of the Convention, concerning the use of French.

(3) For convenience of reference there are set out in Schedules 3D and 3E 3D respectively—

DOI: 10.4324/9781003673194-3

(a) the English text of the 1996 Hague Convention;
(b) the declarations referred to in subsection (2).

3D The 2005 Hague Convention to have the force of law

(1) The 2005 Hague Convention shall have the force of law in the United Kingdom.
(2) For the purposes of this Act the 2005 Hague Convention is to be read together with any reservations or declarations made by the United Kingdom at the time of the approval of the Convention.
(3) For convenience of reference the English text of the 2005 Hague Convention is set out in Schedule 3F.

3E The 2007 Hague Convention to have the force of law

(1) The 2007 Hague Convention shall have the force of law in the United Kingdom.
(2) For the purposes of this Act the 2007 Hague Convention is to be read together with any reservations or declarations made by the United Kingdom at the time of the approval of the Convention.
(3) For convenience of reference the English text of the 2007 Hague Convention is set out in Schedule 3G."
(3) Before Schedule 4 to the 1982 Act insert (as Schedules 3D to 3G) the Schedules set out in Schedules 1 to 4 to this Act.
(4) Schedule 5 (consequential and transitional provision) has effect.

2 *Implementation of other agreements on private international law*

(1) The appropriate national authority may make regulations for the purpose of, or in connection with, implementing any international agreement, as it has effect from time to time, so far as relating to private international law (a "relevant international agreement").
(2) The appropriate national authority may make regulations for the purpose of, or in connection with, applying a relevant international agreement, with or without modifications, as between different jurisdictions within the United Kingdom.
(3) The appropriate national authority may make regulations for the purpose of, or in connection with, giving effect to any arrangements made between—

(a) Her Majesty's government in the United Kingdom, and
(b) the government of a relevant territory,

for applying a relevant international agreement, with or without modifications, as between the United Kingdom, or a jurisdiction within the United Kingdom, and that territory.

(4) Regulations under subsections (1) to (3) may only be made during the operative period.

(5) The operative period is the period of five years beginning with the day on which this Act is passed.

(6) The appropriate national authority in relation to a part of the United Kingdom may by regulations extend the operative period for that part of the United Kingdom by a period of five years.

(7) The power under subsection (6) may be exercised more than once.

(8) The operative period may not be extended for any part of the United Kingdom after it has expired in relation to that part of the United Kingdom.

(9) Regulations under this section may make—

(a) consequential, supplementary, incidental, transitional or saving provision;

(b) different provision for different purposes or for different parts of the United Kingdom.

(10) Regulations under subsections (1) to (3) may include provision about—

(a) enforcement of obligations arising under or by virtue of the regulations;

(b) sharing of information;

(c) legal aid.

(11) Schedule 6 makes further provision about regulations under this section.

(12) In this section—

"appropriate national authority" means—

(a) in relation to England and Wales, the Secretary of State;

(b) in relation to Scotland—

(i) the Scottish Ministers, or

(ii) the Secretary of State acting with the consent of the Scottish Ministers;

(c) in relation to Northern Ireland—

(i) a Northern Ireland department, or

(ii) the Secretary of State acting with the consent of a Northern Ireland department;

"international agreement" means a convention, treaty or other agreement to which the United Kingdom is, or is expected to become, a party;

"private international law" includes rules and other provisions about—

(a) jurisdiction and applicable law;

(b) recognition and enforcement in one country or territory of any of the following that originate in another country or territory—

(i) a judgment, order or arbitral award;

(ii) an agreement, decision or authentic instrument determining or otherwise relating to rights and obligations;

(c) co-operation between judicial or other authorities in different countries or territories in relation to—

(i) service of documents, taking of evidence and other procedures, or

(ii) anything within paragraph (a) or (b);

"relevant international agreement" has the meaning given in subsection (1);

"relevant territory" means—

(a) the Isle of Man;

(b) any of the Channel Islands;

(c) a British overseas territory.

(13) This section and Schedule 6 have effect, with the following modifications, in relation to a model law adopted by an international organisation of which the United Kingdom is a member as they have effect in relation to an international agreement to which the United Kingdom is, or is expected to become, a party.

The modifications are—

(a) a reference in this section or that Schedule to implementing or applying a relevant international agreement is to be read as a reference to giving effect to the model law (with or without modifications);

(b) subsection (1) is to be read as if the words "as revised from time to time" were substituted for the words "as it has effect from time to time".

General

Crown application

Sections 3–4 [Omitted]

Schedules 1–5 [Omitted]

3 Trade Act 2021

Part 1

International trade agreements

1 Implementation of the Agreement on Government Procurement

(1) An appropriate authority may by regulations make such provision as the authority considers appropriate—

(a) for the purpose of implementing the Agreement on Government Procurement signed at Marrakesh on 15 April 1994, as amended on or before the United Kingdom's accession ("the GPA"), or
(b) in consequence of—

(i) the accession of another party to, or the withdrawal of a party from, the GPA,
(ii) a dispute between the United Kingdom and another party to the GPA,
(iii) a modification of another party's Appendix I to the GPA, or
(iv) a modification of the list of central government entities in Annex 1 to the United Kingdom's Appendix I to the GPA.

(2) Regulations under subsection (1) may not come into force before—

(a) in the case of regulations under subsection (1)(a), the day the United Kingdom accedes to the GPA;
(b) in the case of regulations under subsection (1)(b)(i), the day the other party accedes to or, as the case may be, withdraws from, the GPA;
(c) in the case of regulations under subsection (1)(b)(iii) or (iv), the day the modification becomes effective.

(3) Regulations under subsection (1) may make provision modifying assimilated direct principal legislation.
(4) In this section, a "dispute" means a matter in respect of which the United Kingdom or another party is entitled to have recourse to the

DOI: 10.4324/9781003673194-4

Understanding on Rules and Procedures Governing the Settlement of Disputes under Article XX of the GPA.

2 *Implementation of international trade agreements*

(1) An appropriate authority may by regulations make such provision as the authority considers appropriate for the purpose of implementing an international trade agreement to which the United Kingdom is a signatory.

(2) An "international trade agreement" means—

- (a) a free trade agreement, or
- (b) an international agreement that mainly relates to trade, other than a free trade agreement.

(3) Regulations under subsection (1) may make provision for the purpose of implementing a free trade agreement only if the other signatory (or each other signatory) and the European Union were signatories to a free trade agreement immediately before exit day.

(4) Regulations under subsection (1) may make provision for the purpose of implementing an international trade agreement other than a free trade agreement only if the other signatory (or each other signatory) and the European Union were signatories to an international trade agreement immediately before exit day.

(5) If regulations under subsection (1) contain provision about healthcare services, the provision must be consistent with maintaining UK publicly-funded clinical healthcare services.

(6) If regulations under subsection (1) contain provision in any of the areas listed in subsection (7), the provision must be consistent with maintaining UK levels of statutory protection in that area.

(7) The areas referred to in subsection (6) are—

- (a) the protection of human, animal or plant life or health;
- (b) animal welfare;
- (c) environmental protection;
- (d) employment and labour;
- (e) data protection;
- (f) the protection of children and vulnerable adults online.

(8) Regulations under subsection (1) may not make provision that could be made by regulations under section 9 of the Taxation (Cross-border Trade) Act 2018.

(9) Regulations under subsection (1) may, among other things, make provision—

- (a) modifying assimilated direct principal legislation or primary legislation that is assimilated law;

(b) conferring functions on the Secretary of State or any other person, including conferring a discretion but not including a power to make subordinate legislation;
(c) for the delegation of functions;
(d) for civil penalties for failing to comply with the regulations.

(10) No regulations may be made under subsection (1) after the end of—

(a) the period of five years beginning with IP completion day ("the initial five year period"), or
(b) such other period or periods as are specified in regulations made by the Secretary of State in accordance with subsection (11).

(11) Regulations under subsection (10)(b) may not extend the initial five year period, or a further period specified in regulations under that subsection, by more than five years.

(12) In this section—

"UK publicly-funded clinical healthcare services" means publicly-funded clinical healthcare services provided in the United Kingdom, or in the part of the United Kingdom in which the regulations have effect, on the date on which a draft of the regulations is laid;

UK levels of statutory protection" means levels of protection provided by or under—

(a) primary legislation,
(b) subordinate legislation, or
(c) assimilated direct legislation,

which has effect in the United Kingdom, or in the part of the United Kingdom in which the regulations have effect, on the date on which a draft of the regulations is laid.

3 *Free trade agreements and genocide*

(1) Subsection (2) applies if the responsible committee of the House of Commons publishes a report which—

(a) states that there exist credible reports of genocide in the territory of a prospective FTA counter-party, and
(b) confirms that, in preparing the report, the committee has taken such evidence as it considers appropriate.

(2) If, after receiving a response from the Secretary of State, the committee publishes a report which—

(a) includes a statement to the effect that the committee is not satisfied by the Secretary of State's response, and
(b) sets out the wording of a motion to be moved in the House of Commons in accordance with subsection (3),

subsection (3) applies.

(3) A Minister of the Crown must make arrangements for the motion mentioned in subsection (2)(b) to be debated and voted on by the House of Commons.
(4) Subsection (5) applies if the responsible committee of the House of Lords publishes a report which—

(a) states there exist credible reports of genocide in the territory of a prospective FTA counter-party, and
(b) confirms that, in preparing the report, the committee has taken such evidence as it considers appropriate.

(5) If, after receiving a response from the Secretary of State, the committee publishes a statement to the effect that—

(a) it is not satisfied by the Secretary of State's response, and
(b) it seeks a debate on the report,

subsection (6) applies.

(6) A Minister of the Crown must make arrangements for a motion for the House of Lords to take note of the report and the Secretary of State's response to be moved in that House by a Minister of the Crown.
(7) References in this section to genocide are references to genocide occurring, or continuing, after this section comes into force.
(8) In this section—

"genocide" has the same meaning as in the Convention on the Prevention and Punishment of the Crime of Genocide (see Article 2 of the Convention);
"prospective FTA counter-party" means a state with which the United Kingdom is engaged in formal negotiations for a bilateral free trade agreement;
"the responsible committee of the House of Commons" means the select committee of the House of Commons charged with responsibility for this section;
"the responsible committee of the House of Lords" means the select committee of the House of Lords charged with responsibility for this section.

4 Regulations: devolved authorities and general provision

(1) Regulations under section 1(1) or 2(1) may—

(a) make different provision for different purposes or areas;
(b) make provision generally or only in relation to specified cases;
(c) make incidental, supplementary or consequential provision;
(d) make transitional, transitory or saving provision.

(2) Schedule 1 contains restrictions on the exercise of the powers in sections 1(1) and 2(1) by devolved authorities.
(3) Schedule 2 contains provision about the making of regulations under sections 1(1) and 2.
(4) Schedule 3 contains exceptions to restrictions in the devolution settlements for regulations made under section 1(1) or 2(1).

5 Interpretation of Part 1

(1) In this Part—

"appropriate authority" means—

(a) a Minister of the Crown, or
(b) a devolved authority;

"devolved authority" means—

(a) the Scottish Ministers,
(b) the Welsh Ministers, or
(c) a Northern Ireland department;

"free trade agreement" means an agreement that is or was notifiable under—

(a) paragraph 7(a) of Article XXIV of GATT, or
(b) paragraph 7(a) of Article V of GATS;

"GATS" means the General Agreement on Trade in Services, part of Annex 1B to the WTO Agreement (as modified from time to time);
"GATT" means the General Agreement on Tariffs and Trade, part of Annex 1A to the WTO Agreement (as modified from time to time);
"primary legislation" means—

(a) an Act of Parliament,
(b) an Act of the Scottish Parliament,
(c) a Measure or Act of Senedd Cymru, or
(d) Northern Ireland legislation;

"subordinate legislation" has the meaning given in section 20(1) of the European Union (Withdrawal) Act 2018;

"the WTO Agreement" means the agreement establishing the World Trade Organisation signed at Marrakesh on 15 April 1994.

(2) In this Part a reference to being a signatory to an international trade agreement includes a reference to—

(a) exchanging instruments, where the exchange constitutes the agreement;
(b) acceding to the agreement.

(3) In this Part a reference to a draft of regulations being laid is a reference to a draft of the regulations, or a draft of the instrument containing the regulations, being laid before—

(a) each House of Parliament, in the case of regulations to which paragraph 4(1) or 5 of Schedule 2 applies;
(b) the Scottish Parliament, in the case of regulations to which paragraph 4(2) of Schedule 2 applies;
(c) Senedd Cymru, in the case of regulations to which paragraph 4(3) of Schedule 2 applies;
(d) the Northern Ireland Assembly, in the case of regulations to which paragraph 4(4) of Schedule 2 applies.

(4) … [Words in s. 5(4) omitted]
(5) In this section, "domestic law" means the law of England and Wales, Scotland or Northern Ireland.

Part 2

The Trade Remedies Authority

6 The Trade Remedies Authority

(1) A body corporate called the Trade Remedies Authority ("the TRA") is established.
(2) Schedule 4 contains further provision about the TRA.
(3) Schedule 5 contains provision about schemes for the transfer of staff in connection with the establishment of the TRA.

7 Provision of advice, support and assistance by the TRA

(1) The TRA must provide the Secretary of State with such advice, support and assistance as the Secretary of State requests in connection with—

(a) the conduct of an international trade dispute,

(b) functions of the Secretary of State relating to trade, and
(c) functions of the TRA.

(2) Advice, support and assistance requested under subsection (1) may include, among other things—

(a) analysis of trade remedy measures imposed in countries or territories other than the United Kingdom, and
(b) analysis of the impact of such measures on producers and exporters in the United Kingdom.

(3) Before making a request under subsection (1), the Secretary of State must—

(a) consult the TRA, and
(b) have regard to the expertise of the TRA and to the need to protect—

(i) its operational independence, and
(ii) its ability to make impartial assessments when performing its functions.

(4) The TRA may otherwise provide such advice, support and assistance as it considers appropriate in relation to—

(a) international trade, and
(b) trade remedies.

Part 3 [Omitted]

Part 4 [Omitted]

Part 5

General

16 Interpretation

In this Act—

"devolved authority" has the meaning given in section 5(1);
"Minister of the Crown" has the same meaning as in the Ministers of the Crown Act 1975;
"modify" includes amend, repeal or revoke (and related expressions are to be read accordingly).

17 Extent

(1) Subject to subsection (2), this Act extends to England and Wales, Scotland and Northern Ireland.
(2) Any provision of this Act which amends an enactment has the same extent as the enactment amended.

18 Commencement [Omitted]

19 Short title [Omitted]

Schedules 1–3 [Omitted]

Schedule 4

The Trade Remedies Authority

Status

1 (1) The TRA is not to be regarded—

(a) as the servant or agent of the Crown, or
(b) as enjoying any status, immunity or privilege of the Crown.

(2) The TRA's property is not to be regarded—

(a) as the property of the Crown, or
(b) as property held on behalf of the Crown.

Membership

2 (1) The TRA is to consist of—

(a) a Chair appointed by the Secretary of State,
(b) other non-executive members appointed by the Secretary of State,
(c) a chief executive appointed by the Chair with the approval of the Secretary of State or, if the first Chair has not been appointed, by the Secretary of State, and
(d) other executive members appointed by the Chair.

(2) The total number of members must not exceed nine.
(3) The Secretary of State must consult the Chair before appointing the other non-executive members.

(4) The Secretary of State and the Chair must ensure, so far as practicable, that the number of non-executive members is at all times greater than the number of executive members.

Terms of appointment and tenure of members

3 A person holds and vacates office as a member of the TRA in accordance with the terms and conditions of the person's appointment.

4 The terms and conditions of a person's appointment as a non-executive member of the TRA are to be determined by the Secretary of State; but that is subject to the following provisions of this Schedule.

5 The terms and conditions of a person's appointment as an executive member of the TRA are to be determined by the Chair with the approval of the Secretary of State; but that is subject to the following provisions of this Schedule.

6 The terms and conditions of a person's appointment may cover, among other things—

(a) the period for which the person is to hold office;
(b) the person's eligibility for re-appointment;
(c) circumstances in which a person's membership may be suspended.

7 A person may resign from office as a non-executive member of the TRA by notifying the Secretary of State.

8 A person may resign from office as an executive member of the TRA by notifying the Chair.

9 The Secretary of State may remove a person from office as a non-executive member of the TRA if, in the opinion of the Secretary of State, the person is unable or unfit to carry out the functions of the office.

10 The Chair may remove a person from office as an executive member of the TRA if, in the opinion of the Chair, the person is unable or unfit to carry out the functions of the office.

Remuneration of members

11 The TRA must pay to non-executive members of the TRA such remuneration as the Secretary of State may determine.

12 The TRA must pay to executive members of the TRA such remuneration as the Chair may determine with the approval of the Secretary of State.

13 The TRA must pay, or make provision for paying, to or in respect of any person who is or has been a non-executive member of the TRA, such sums as the Secretary of State may determine in respect of allowances, expenses and gratuities.

14 The TRA must pay, or make provision for paying, to or in respect of any person who is or has been an executive member of the TRA, such sums as the Chair may determine with the approval of the Secretary of State in respect of pension, allowances, expenses and gratuities.

15 If a person ceases to be a non-executive member of the TRA and the Secretary of State determines that the person should be compensated because of special circumstances, the TRA must pay compensation of such amount as the Secretary of State may determine.

16 If a person ceases to be an executive member of the TRA and the Chair determines with the approval of the Secretary of State that the person should be compensated because of special circumstances, the TRA must pay compensation of such amount as the Chair may, with the approval of the Secretary of State, determine.

A chief executive appointed by the Secretary of State

17 Paragraphs 18 to 23 apply in respect of a person who is appointed as chief executive by the Secretary of State under paragraph 2(1)(c).

18 The terms and conditions of a person's appointment as chief executive are to be determined by the Secretary of State; but that is subject to the other provisions of this Schedule.

19 If the first Chair has not been appointed, a person appointed as chief executive may resign from office by notifying the Secretary of State.

20 The Secretary of State may remove a person from office as the chief executive if—

(a) the first Chair has not been appointed, and
(b) in the opinion of the Secretary of State, the person is unable or unfit to carry out the functions of the office.

21 The TRA must pay to a person appointed as chief executive—

(a) such remuneration as the Secretary of State may determine, or
(b) following the appointment of the first Chair, such remuneration as the Chair may determine with the approval of the Secretary of State.

22 The TRA must pay, or make provision for paying, to or in respect of a person who is or has been the chief executive—

(a) such sums in respect of pension, allowances, expenses and gratuities as the Secretary of State may determine, or
(b) following appointment of the first Chair, such sums in respect of pension, allowances, expenses and gratuities as the Chair may determine with the approval of the Secretary of State.

23 If a person ceases to be the chief executive of the TRA at a time when the first Chair has not been appointed and the Secretary of State determines

that the person should be compensated because of special circumstances, the TRA must pay compensation of such amount as the Secretary of State may determine.

Staffing of the TRA

24 (1) The TRA may—

(a) appoint employees, and
(b) make such other arrangements for the staffing of the TRA as it considers appropriate.

(2) The terms and conditions of appointment as an employee are to be determined by the TRA.
(3) The TRA may pay its employees such remuneration as the TRA may determine.
(4) The TRA may pay, or make provision for paying, to or in respect of any person who is or has been an employee of the TRA, such sums as the TRA may determine in respect of pension, allowances, expenses or gratuities.
(5) In the Superannuation Act 1972 ("the 1972 Act"), in Schedule 1 (kinds of employment to which a scheme under section 1 of the 1972 Act can apply), in the list of "Other Bodies", at the appropriate place insert— "Trade Remedies Authority."
(6) The TRA must pay to the Minister for the Civil Service, at such times as the Minister may direct, such sums as the Minister may determine in respect of any increase attributable to sub-paragraph (5) in the sums payable out of money provided by Parliament under the 1972 Act.
(7) Sub-paragraphs (1) to (4) apply in respect of employees that are not executive members of the TRA.

Committees

25 (1) The TRA may establish committees, and any committee so established may establish sub-committees.
(2) A committee or sub-committee so established is referred to in this Schedule as a "TRA committee".
(3) A TRA committee may consist of or include persons who are neither members, nor employees, of the TRA.
(4) The TRA must pay such allowances as it may determine to any person who—

(a) is a member of a TRA committee, but
(b) is neither a member, nor an employee, of the TRA.

(5) The TRA must keep under review—

(a) the structure of the TRA committees, and
(b) the scope of each committee's activities.

Procedure

26 The TRA may determine its own procedure and the procedure of any TRA committee (including quorum).

Delegation of functions

28 (1) The TRA may delegate any of its functions to—

(a) a member of the TRA,
(b) an employee, or other member of staff, authorised for that purpose, or
(c) a TRA committee.

(2) But a function may not be delegated to a committee that includes a person who is neither a member, nor an employee, of the TRA insofar as the function could be exercised in relation to a specific trade remedies investigation.
(3) Otherwise, a function is delegated under this paragraph to the extent, and on the terms, that the TRA determines.
(4) In this Schedule "trade remedies investigation" means an investigation by the TRA under provision made by or under Part 1 of the Taxation (Cross-border Trade) Act 2018.

Funding

29 The Secretary of State must pay to the TRA such sums as the Secretary of State considers appropriate for the purpose of enabling the TRA to perform its functions.

Accounts and audit

30 (1) The TRA must—

(a) keep proper accounts and proper records in relation to them, and
(b) prepare a statement of accounts in respect of each financial year.

(2) The statement of accounts must comply with any directions given by the Secretary of State with the approval of the Treasury as to—

(a) its content and form;
(b) the methods and principles to be applied in preparing it;

(c) the additional information (if any) which is to be provided for the information of Parliament.

(3) The TRA must send a copy of the statement of accounts to the Secretary of State and the Comptroller and Auditor General as soon as reasonably practicable after the end of the financial year to which it relates.

(4) The Comptroller and Auditor General must—

(a) examine, certify and report on each statement of accounts, and
(b) send a copy of each report and certified statement to the Secretary of State.

(5) The Secretary of State must lay before Parliament a copy of each such report and certified statement.

(6) The chief executive of the TRA is to be its accounting officer.

(7) In this Schedule "financial year" means—

(a) the period beginning with the date on which the TRA is established and ending with the second 31 March following that date, and
(b) each successive period of 12 months.

Annual report

31 (1) The TRA must prepare a report on the performance of its functions during each financial year.

(2) The report must include the statement of accounts in respect of that year.

(3) The report must be prepared as soon as reasonably practicable after the end of the financial year to which it relates.

(4) The TRA must send the report to the Secretary of State.

(5) The Secretary of State must lay the report before Parliament.

Seal and evidence

32 (1) The application of the TRA's seal must be authenticated by the signature of—

(a) a member of the TRA, or
(b) an employee of the TRA authorised for that purpose.

(2) A document purporting to be duly executed under the TRA's seal or signed on its behalf—

(a) is to be received in evidence, and
(b) is to be taken to be executed or signed in that way, unless the contrary is shown.

(3) This paragraph does not apply in Scotland.

Supplementary powers

33 (1) The TRA may do anything which appears to it to be necessary or expedient for the purpose of, or in connection with, the performance of its functions.

(2) Under sub-paragraph (1), the TRA may among other things—

(a) acquire and dispose of land and other property,
(b) enter into contracts, and
(c) accept gifts of money, land or other property.

Guidance

34 (1) In performing its functions, the TRA must have regard to guidance published by the Secretary of State.

(2) Sub-paragraph (1) does not apply in respect of an ongoing trade remedies investigation if the guidance is published during that investigation.

(3) Before publishing guidance, the Secretary of State must—

(a) consult the TRA, and
(b) have regard to the expertise of the TRA and to the need to protect—
   (i) its operational independence, and
   (ii) its ability to make impartial assessments when performing its functions.

(4) In particular, the Secretary of State may not publish guidance in relation to a specific trade remedies investigation.

Public records

35 In Part 2 of the Table in paragraph 3 of Schedule 1 to the Public Records Act 1958 (definition of public records), at the appropriate place insert— "Trade Remedies Authority."

Investigation by the Parliamentary Commissioner

36 In Schedule 2 to the Parliamentary Commissioner Act 1967 (departments subject to investigation), at the appropriate place insert— "Trade Remedies Authority."

House of Commons disqualification

37 In Part 2 of Schedule 1 to the House of Commons Disqualification Act 1975 (bodies of which members are disqualified), at the appropriate place insert— "The Trade Remedies Authority."

Northern Ireland Assembly disqualification

38 In Part 2 of Schedule 1 to the Northern Ireland Assembly Disqualification Act 1975 (bodies of which members are disqualified), at the appropriate place insert— "The Trade Remedies Authority."

Freedom of information

39 In Part 6 of Schedule 1 to the Freedom of Information Act 2000 (public authorities to which this Act applies), at the appropriate place insert— "The Trade Remedies Authority."

Public sector equality duty

40 In Part 1 of Schedule 19 to the Equality Act 2010 (authorities subject to the public sector equality duty), in the group of entries under the heading "Industry, Business, Finance etc", at the appropriate place insert— "The Trade Remedies Authority."

Schedules 5–6 [Omitted]

4 Electronic Trade Documents Act 2023

1 Definition of "paper trade document"

(1) A document is a "paper trade document" for the purposes of this Act if—

(a) it is in paper form,
(b) it is a document of a type commonly used in at least one part of the United Kingdom in connection with—

(i) trade in or transport of goods, or
(ii) financing such trade or transport, and

(c) possession of the document is required as a matter of law or commercial custom, usage or practice for a person to claim performance of an obligation.

(2) The following are examples of documents that are commonly used as mentioned in subsection (1)(b)—

(a) a bill of exchange;
(b) a promissory note;
(c) a bill of lading;
(d) a ship's delivery order;
(e) a warehouse receipt;
(f) a mate's receipt;
(g) a marine insurance policy;
(h) a cargo insurance certificate.

2 Definition of "electronic trade document"

(1) This section applies where information in electronic form is information that, if contained in a document in paper form, would lead to the document being a paper trade document.
(2) The information, together with any other information with which it is logically associated that is also in electronic form, constitutes an

DOI: 10.4324/9781003673194-5

"electronic trade document" for the purposes of this Act if a reliable system is used to—

(a) identify the document so that it can be distinguished from any copies,
(b) protect the document against unauthorised alteration,
(c) secure that it is not possible for more than one person to exercise control of the document at any one time,
(d) allow any person who is able to exercise control of the document to demonstrate that the person is able to do so, and
(e) secure that a transfer of the document has effect to deprive any person who was able to exercise control of the document immediately before the transfer of the ability to do so (unless the person is able to exercise control by virtue of being a transferee).

(3) For the purposes of subsection (2)—

(a) a person exercises control of a document when the person uses, transfers or otherwise disposes of the document (whether or not the person has a legal right to do so), and
(b) persons acting jointly are to be treated as one person.

(4) Reading or viewing a document is not, of itself, sufficient to amount to use of the document for the purposes of subsection (3)(a).

(5) When determining whether a system is reliable for the purposes of subsection (2), the matters that may be taken into account include—

(a) any rules of the system that apply to its operation;
(b) any measures taken to secure the integrity of information held on the system;
(c) any measures taken to prevent unauthorised access to and use of the system;
(d) the security of the hardware and software used by the system;
(e) the regularity of and extent of any audit of the system by an independent body;
(f) any assessment of the reliability of the system made by a body with supervisory or regulatory functions;
(g) the provisions of any voluntary scheme or industry standard that apply in relation to the system.

3 Possession, indorsement and effect of electronic trade documents

(1) A person may possess, indorse and part with possession of an electronic trade document.

(2) An electronic trade document has the same effect as an equivalent paper trade document.

(3) Anything done in relation to an electronic trade document has the same effect (if any) in relation to the document as it would have in relation to an equivalent paper trade document.

(4) An electronic trade document is to be treated as corporeal moveable property for the purposes of any Act of the Scottish Parliament relating to the creation of a security in the form of a pledge over moveable property.

4 Change of form

(1) A paper trade document may be converted into an electronic trade document, and an electronic trade document may be converted into a paper trade document, if (and only if)—

(a) a statement that the document has been converted is included in the document in its new form, and

(b) any contractual or other requirements relating to the conversion of the document are complied with.

(2) Where a document is converted in accordance with subsection (1)—

(a) the document in its old form ceases to have effect, and

(b) all rights and liabilities relating to the document continue to have effect in relation to the document in its new form.

5 Exceptions

(1) If an intention that section 3 should not apply in relation to an electronic trade document appears in, or can reasonably be inferred from, the document or terms that have effect in relation to the document—

(a) that section does not apply in relation to the document, and (b) section 4 also does not apply in relation to it.

(2) Sections 1 to 4 do not apply in relation to—

(a) an uncertificated unit of a security that is transferable by means of a relevant system in accordance with the Uncertificated Securities Regulations 2001 (S.I. 2001/3755), or

(b) a document or instrument of a type specified in regulations made by the appropriate authority.

(3) The Secretary of State may by regulations amend this section so as to amend or remove the exception conferred by subsection (2)(a).

(4) The Secretary of State must consult the Scottish Ministers before making regulations under subsection (2)(b) that contain provision that is to have effect in relation to Scotland.

(5) Subsection (4) does not apply if the regulations are to be made by the Secretary of State and the Scottish Ministers acting jointly.

(6) Regulations under this section may include incidental, consequential, transitional or saving provision.

(7) "The appropriate authority", in relation to regulations under subsection (2)(b), means—

(a) in any case, the Secretary of State or the Secretary of State and the Scottish Ministers acting jointly;

(b) in a case in which all of the provision made by the regulations is within Scottish devolved competence, the Scottish Ministers.

(8) Provision is within Scottish devolved competence if it is provision which would be within the legislative competence of the Scottish Parliament if contained in an Act of that Parliament.

6 Regulations under section 5

[Omitted]

7 Consequential provision

(1) In section 89B(2) of the Bills of Exchange Act 1882 (instruments to which section 89A applies), at the end insert "or to anything that is an electronic trade document for the purposes of the Electronic Trade Documents Act 2023 (see section 2 of that Act)."

(2) In section 1 of the Carriage of Goods by Sea Act 1992 (shipping documents etc), omit subsections (5) and (6).

8 Extent, commencement and short title

(1) This Act extends to England and Wales, Scotland and Northern Ireland, except that section 3(4) extends only to Scotland.

(2) [Omitted].

(3) Sections 3 and 4 do not apply in relation to a paper trade document or an electronic trade document issued before the day on which this Act comes into force.

(4) [Omitted].

5 Retained EU Law (Revocation and Reform) Act 2023

Sunsets of retained EU law

1 Sunset of EU-derived subordinate legislation and retained direct EU legislation

(1) Legislation listed in Schedule 1 is revoked at the end of 2023, to the extent specified there.

(2) In that Schedule—

(a) Part 1 lists subordinate legislation;
(b) Part 2 lists retained direct EU legislation.

(3) The revocation of an instrument, or a provision of an instrument, by subsection (1) does not affect an amendment made by the instrument or provision to any other enactment.

(4) Subsection (1) does not apply to anything specified in regulations made by a relevant national authority.

(5) No regulations may be made under subsection (4) after 31 October 2023.

2 Sunset of retained EU rights, powers, liabilities etc.

(1) Section 4 of the European Union (Withdrawal) Act 2018 (saving for rights, powers, liabilities etc. under section 2(1) of the European Communities Act 1972) is repealed at the end of 2023.

(2) Accordingly, anything which, immediately before the end of 2023, is retained EU law by virtue of that section is not recognised or available in domestic law at or after that time (and, accordingly, is not to be enforced, allowed or followed).

Assimilation of retained EU law

3 Abolition of supremacy of EU law

(1) In section 5 of the European Union (Withdrawal) Act 2018 (exceptions to savings and incorporation), before subsection (1) insert—

DOI: 10.4324/9781003673194-6

"(A1) The principle of the supremacy of EU law is not part of domestic law. This applies after the end of 2023, in relation to any enactment or rule of law (whenever passed or made).

(A2) Any provision of retained direct EU legislation—

(a) must, so far as possible, be read and given effect in a way which is compatible with all domestic enactments, and
(b) is subject to all domestic enactments, so far as it is incompatible with them.

(A3) Subsection (A2) is subject to—

(a) section 186 of the Data Protection Act 2018 (data subject's rights and other prohibitions and restrictions);
(b) regulations under section 7(1) of the Retained EU Law (Revocation and Reform) Act 2023."

(2) In that section, at the end insert—

"(8) In this section "domestic enactment" means an enactment other than one consisting of retained direct EU legislation."

(3) In consequence of subsection (1), the European Union (Withdrawal) Act 2018 is amended as follows—

(a) in section 5—

(i) omit subsections (1) to (3);
(ii) in subsection (7), for "(1)" substitute "(A1)";

(b) in section 7(5)(a), for "(1) to (3)" substitute "(A1) to (A3)";
(c) in Schedule 1 omit paragraph 5(2).

4 *Abolition of general principles of EU law*

(1) The European Union (Withdrawal) Act 2018 is amended as follows.
(2) In section 5 (exceptions to savings and incorporation)—

(a) after subsection (A3) (inserted by section 3(1)) insert—

"(A4) No general principle of EU law is part of domestic law after the end of 2023.";

(b) omit subsection (5).

(3) In section 6 (interpretation)—

(a) in subsection (3)(a) omit "and any retained general principles of EU law";
(b) in subsection (7) omit the definition of "retained general principles of EU law".

(4) In section 7(5)(b) (status of retained EU law) omit "and retained general principles of EU law".

(5) In section 21(1) (index of defined expressions), in the table, omit the entry for "Retained general principles of EU law".

(6) In Schedule 1 (further provision about exceptions to savings and incorporation) omit paragraphs 2 and 3 (general principles of EU law) and the italic heading before them.

(7) In paragraph 39 of Schedule 8 (transitional provision relating to certain exceptions to savings and incorporation)—

(a) in sub-paragraph (1) for "1 to 4" substitute "1 and 4";
(b) in sub-paragraph (2) for "1 to 4" substitute "1 and 4";
(c) in sub-paragraph (3) for "paragraphs 3 and" substitute "paragraph";
(d) in sub-paragraph (4) for "1 to 4" substitute "1 and 4";
(e) omit sub-paragraphs (5) and (6).

5 *"Assimilated law"*

(1) As regards all times after the end of 2023, the things listed in the left-hand column are to be known by the names in the right-hand column.

At or before the end of 2023	*After the end of 2023*
Retained EU law	Assimilated law
Retained case law	Assimilated case law
Retained direct EU legislation	Assimilated direct legislation
Retained direct minor EU legislation	Assimilated direct minor legislation
Retained direct principal EU legislation	Assimilated direct principal legislation
Retained domestic case law	Assimilated domestic case law
Retained EU case law	Assimilated EU case law
Retained EU obligation	Assimilated obligation
Retained EU law governing the CAP direct payment schemes	Assimilated law governing the CAP direct payment schemes
Retained direct EU CAP legislation	Assimilated direct CAP legislation

(2) Accordingly, as regards all times at or before the end of 2023, the things listed in the right-hand column continue to be known by the names in the left-hand column.

(3) Schedule 2 contains amendments consequential on subsection (1).

(4) A reference in an enactment to a thing in the left-hand column of the table in subsection (1) is to be read, as regards all times after the end of 2023, as a reference to the thing by its name in the right-hand column.

(5) Subsection (4) does not apply to any title of an enactment (including any provision about how an enactment may be cited) or any reference to a title of an enactment.

(6) The provision that may be made by regulations under section 19 (power to make consequential provision) in consequence of subsection (1) of this section includes, in particular—

(a) provision adding entries to the table in subsection (1) for things which relate to the things for which there are entries in the table (and adding definitions for those things to subsection (7));

(b) provision amending an enactment in consequence of the name of a thing being changed by subsection (1) (including by virtue of regulations under section 19).

(7) In this section—

"retained case law", "retained domestic case law" and "retained EU case law" have the meaning given by section 6(7) of the European Union (Withdrawal) Act 2018 (as it has effect on the day on which this Act is passed);

"retained EU law", "retained direct EU legislation", "retained direct minor EU legislation", "retained direct principal EU legislation" and "retained EU obligation" have the meaning given by Schedule 1 to the Interpretation Act 1978 (as it has effect on the day on which this Act is passed);

"retained EU law governing the CAP direct payment schemes" and "retained direct EU CAP legislation" have the meaning given by section 2 of the Direct Payments to Farmers (Legislative Continuity) Act 2020 (as it has effect on the day on which this Act is passed).

Interpretation and effect of retained EU law

6 Role of courts

(1) Section 6 of the European Union (Withdrawal) Act 2018 (interpretation of retained EU law) is amended as specified in subsections (2) to (7).

(2) In subsection (4) (courts not bound by retained case law)—

(a) in paragraph (b)—

(i) in sub-paragraph (i) omit the words from "otherwise" to "1998)";

(ii) after sub-paragraph (ii) (and on a new line) insert "(except, when sitting as a court of appeal in relation to a compatibility issue or devolution issue, so far as there is relevant domestic case law which modifies or applies the retained EU case law and is binding on the court);";

(b) for paragraph (ba) substitute—

"(ba) a relevant appeal court is not bound by any retained EU case law (except so far as there is relevant domestic case law which modifies or applies the retained EU case law and is binding on the relevant appeal court), and";

(c) after paragraph (c) (and on a new line) insert "and see also subsection (5ZA) below and sections 6A to 6C."

(3) For subsection (5) substitute—

"(5) In deciding whether to depart from any retained EU case law by virtue of subsection (4)(a), (b) or (ba), the higher court concerned must (among other things) have regard to—

(a) the fact that decisions of a foreign court are not (unless otherwise provided) binding;
(b) any changes of circumstances which are relevant to the retained EU case law;
(c) the extent to which the retained EU case law restricts the proper development of domestic law."

(4) After that subsection insert—

"(5ZA) A higher court may depart from its own retained domestic case law if it considers it right to do so having regard (among other things) to—

(a) the extent to which the retained domestic case law is determined or influenced by retained EU case law from which the court has departed or would depart;
(b) any changes of circumstances which are relevant to the retained domestic case law;
(c) the extent to which the retained domestic case law restricts the proper development of domestic law."

(5) Omit subsections (5A) to (5D) (power to make regulations about which courts or tribunals are bound by retained EU case law).

(6) After subsection (6A) insert—

"(6B) In this section—

"compatibility issue" has the meaning given by section 288ZA(2) of the Criminal Procedure (Scotland) Act 1995;

"devolution issue" has the meaning given by paragraph 1 of Schedule 6 to the Scotland Act 1998;

"relevant appeal court" means—

(a) the Court Martial Appeal Court,
(b) the Court of Appeal in England and Wales,
(c) the Inner House of the Court of Session,
(d) the court for hearing appeals under section 57(1)(b) of the Representation of the People Act 1983,
(e) the Lands Valuation Appeal Court, or
(f) the Court of Appeal in Northern Ireland;

"relevant domestic case law" means any principles laid down by, and any decisions of, a court or tribunal in the United Kingdom, as they have effect on or after IP completion day."

(7) In subsection (7) before the definition of "retained case law" insert—
""higher court" means—

(a) the Supreme Court,
(b) the High Court of Justiciary when sitting as mentioned in subsection (4)(b)(i) or (ii), or
(c) a relevant appeal court;".

(8) After section 6 of that Act insert—

"6A References on retained case law by lower courts or tribunals

(1) A court or tribunal (other than a higher court) may refer one or more points of law which arise on retained case law and are relevant to proceedings before it if—

(a) it is bound by the retained case law, and
(b) it considers that the point or points of law are of general public importance.

(2) A court or tribunal may make a reference—

(a) of its own motion, or
(b) pursuant to an application made by a party to the proceedings.

(3) A reference is to be made—

(a) in the case of a reference concerning (wholly or in part) retained case law of the Supreme Court, to that court;
(b) in any other case, to the appropriate appeal court

(4) Where a single point of law is referred to a court, the court may accept the reference if it considers that the point of law—

(a) is relevant to the proceedings, and
(b) is of general public importance.

(5) Where two or more points of law are referred to a court, the court may accept the reference so far as relating to a point of law which the court considers meets the conditions in subsection (4)(a) and (b).

(6) A court which has accepted a reference must decide the point or points of law concerned; and the court or tribunal which made the reference must apply that decision so far as relevant to the proceedings before it.

(7) No appeal may be made from a decision of a court or tribunal—

(a) to make, or not to make, a reference, or
(b) to accept or refuse a reference.

(8) An appeal from a decision of the appropriate appeal court under subsection (6) may, with permission, be made to the Supreme Court.

(9) In this section—

"the appropriate appeal court" means, in relation to proceedings before a court or tribunal, the court mentioned in subsection (10) to which an appeal from the court or tribunal in those proceedings on the point of law (or an appeal at any remove from that appeal) would lie; "permission" means permission granted by the court making the decision or by the Supreme Court.

(10) The courts referred to in subsection (9) are—

(a) the Court Martial Appeal Court;
(b) the Court of Appeal in England and Wales;
(c) the Inner House of the Court of Session;
(d) the High Court of Justiciary when sitting as a court of appeal or on a reference under section 123(1) of the Criminal Procedure (Scotland) Act 1995;
(e) the court for hearing appeals under section 57(1)(b) of the Representation of the People Act 1983;
(f) the Lands Valuation Appeal Court;
(g) the Court of Appeal in Northern Ireland.

6B References on retained case law by law officers

(1) This section applies where—

(a) proceedings before a court or tribunal (other than a higher court) have concluded,
(b) no reference was made under section 6A in relation to the proceedings, and
(c) either—

(i) there has been no appeal, or
(ii) any appeal has been finally dealt with otherwise than by a higher court.

(2) The following may refer a point of law which was relevant to the proceedings and arises on retained case law—

(a) any UK law officer;
(b) the Lord Advocate, if the point of law relates to the meaning or effect of relevant Scotland legislation;
(c) the Counsel General for Wales, if the point of law relates to the meaning or effect of relevant Wales legislation;
(d) the Attorney General for Northern Ireland, if the point of law relates to the meaning or effect of relevant Northern Ireland legislation.

(3) A reference must be made within the period of 6 months beginning with—

(a) if there has been no appeal, the last day on which an appeal could have been made;
(b) otherwise, the day on which the appeal was finally dealt with.

(4) A reference is to be made—

(a) in the case of a reference concerning (wholly or in part) retained-case law of theSupreme Court, to that court;
(b) in any other case, to the appropriate appeal court (as defined by section 6A).

(5) The court to which the reference is made must accept the reference, and decide the point or points of law concerned.
(6) Any such decision does not affect the outcome of the proceedings mentioned in subsection (1).
(7) An appeal from a decision of the appropriate appeal court under subsection (5) may, with permission, be made to the Supreme Court.
(8) In this section—

"permission" means permission granted by the court making the decision or by the Supreme Court;
"relevant Northern Ireland legislation" means—

(a) Northern Ireland legislation,
(b) subordinate legislation made by a Northern Ireland devolved authority acting alone,
(c) anything inserted into an enactment by legislation within paragraph (a) or (b), or

(d) any other provision of an enactment if—

(i) the provision would be within the legislative competence of the Northern Ireland Assembly if it were contained in an Act of that Assembly and the provision would not, if it were contained in a Bill in the Northern Ireland Assembly, result in the Bill requiring the consent of the Secretary of State under section 8 of the Northern Ireland Act 1998, or

(ii) it is provision which could be made in other subordinate legislation by any Northern Ireland devolved authority acting alone;

"relevant Scotland legislation" means—

(a) an Act of the Scottish Parliament,

(b) subordinate legislation made by the Scottish Ministers, the First Minister or the Lord Advocate acting alone,

(c) anything inserted into an enactment by legislation within paragraph (a) or (b), or

(d) any other provision of an enactment if—

(i) the provision would be within the legislative competence of the Scottish Parliament if it were contained in an Act of that Parliament, or

(ii) it is provision which could be made in other subordinate legislation by the Scottish Ministers, the First Minister or the Lord Advocate acting alone;

"relevant Wales legislation" means—

(a) an Act or Measure of Senedd Cymru,

(b) subordinate legislation made by the Welsh Ministers acting alone or the National Assembly for Wales constituted by the Government of Wales Act 1998,

(c) anything inserted into an enactment by legislation within paragraph (a) or (b), or

(d) any other provision of an enactment if—

(i) the provision would be within the legislative competence of Senedd Cymru if it were contained in an Act of the Senedd (ignoring any requirement for consent of a Minister of the Crown imposed under Schedule 7B to the Government of Wales Act 2006), or

(ii) it is provision which could be made in other subordinate legislation by the Welsh Ministers acting alone;

"UK law officer" means the Attorney General for England and Wales, the Advocate General for Scotland or the Advocate General for Northern Ireland.

(9) For the purposes of subsections (1)(c)(i) and (3), ignore the possibility of an appeal out of time.

6C Interventions on retained case law by law officers

(1) This section applies where a higher court is considering any argument made by a party to proceedings that the court should depart from retained case law.

(2) The following are entitled to notice of the proceedings—

(a) each UK law officer;
(b) the Lord Advocate;
(c) the Counsel General for Wales;
(d) the Attorney General for Northern Ireland.

(3) The following are entitled to be joined as a party to the proceedings on giving notice to the court—

(a) any UK law officer;
(b) the Lord Advocate, if the argument relates to the meaning or effect of relevant Scotland legislation;
(c) the Counsel General for Wales, if the argument relates to the meaning or effect of relevant Wales legislation;
(d) the Attorney General for Northern Ireland, if the argument relates to the meaning or effect of relevant Northern Ireland legislation.

(4) Notice under subsection (3) may be given at any time during the proceedings.

(5) In this section, "relevant Northern Ireland legislation", "relevant Scotland legislation", "relevant Wales legislation" and "UK law officer" have the meaning given by section 6B."

(9) In section 21(1) of that Act (index of defined expressions), in the Table after the entry for "Future relationship agreement" insert—

"Higher court	*Section 6(7)".*

(10) In section 60A of the Competition Act 1998 (principles etc. to be applied in relation to competition decisions) after subsection (9) insert—

"(10) Section 6(2) to (6) of the European Union (Withdrawal) Act 2018 (which make provision similar to that made by this section) do not apply."

7 *Compatibility*

(1) A relevant national authority may by regulations provide that subsection (2) applies (and section 5(A2) of the European Union (Withdrawal) Act 2018 does not apply) to the relationship between—

(a) any domestic enactment specified in the regulations, and
(b) any provision of assimilated direct EU legislation so specified.

(2) Where this subsection applies, the domestic enactment specified under subsection (1)(a)—

(a) must, so far as possible, be read and given effect in a way which is compatible with the provision of assimilated direct EU legislation specified under subsection (1)(b), and
(b) is subject to that provision of assimilated direct EU legislation so far as it is incompatible with it.

(3) Regulations under subsection (1) may make provision by modifying any enactment.
(4) No regulations may be made under subsection (1) after 23 June 2026.
(5) In this section "domestic enactment" has the same meaning as in section 5 of the European Union (Withdrawal) Act 2018.

8 *Incompatibility orders*

After section 6C of the European Union (Withdrawal) Act 2018 (inserted by section 6 of this Act) insert—

"6D Incompatibility orders

(1) This section applies if a court or tribunal decides, in the course of any proceedings—

(a) that a provision of retained direct EU legislation is incompatible with, and by virtue of section 5(A2)(b) subject to, any domestic enactment, or
(b) that a domestic enactment is incompatible with, and by virtue of section 7(1) of the Retained EU Law (Revocation and Reform) Act 2023 subject to, a provision of retained direct EU legislation.

(2) The court or tribunal must make an order (an "incompatibility order") to that effect (in addition to any exercise of other powers that it may have in relation to the proceedings).
(3) An incompatibility order may (among other things)—

(a) set out the effect of the relevant provision in its operation in relation to that particular case;
(b) delay the coming into force of the order;
(c) remove or limit any effect of the operation of the relevant provision before the coming into force of the order.

(4) Provision included in an incompatibility order may be made subject to conditions.
(5) In this section—

"domestic enactment" has the same meaning as in section 5 of this Act;

"the relevant provision" means section 5(A2)(b) of this Act or section 7(1) of the Retained EU Law (Revocation and Reform) Act 2023 (as the case may be)." Modification of retained EU law

9 *Scope of powers*

(1) Part 1 of Schedule 8 to the European Union (Withdrawal) Act 2018 (general consequential provision) is amended as specified in subsections (2) to (7).
(2) In paragraph 3 (existing powers to make subordinate legislation etc: modifications)—

(a) in sub-paragraph (1) omit paragraph (b) (and the "and" immediately before it);
(b) omit sub-paragraph (2).

(3) In paragraph 4 (procedure for existing powers to make subordinate legislation etc)—

(a) omit sub-paragraphs (1) to (5);
(b) before sub-paragraph (6) insert—

"(5A) Any subordinate legislation which is (or is to be) made, confirmed or approved by virtue of paragraph 3 is subject to the same procedure (if any) before Parliament, the Scottish Parliament, Senedd Cymru or the Northern Ireland Assembly as would apply to that legislation if it were amending or revoking an enactment contained in subordinate legislation made under a different power.";

(c) in sub-paragraph (9) omit "amending or repealing an enactment contained in primary legislation or" and "amending or repealing or (as the case may be)";
(d) omit sub-paragraph (10).

(4) Omit paragraphs 5 and 6.
(5) Omit paragraphs 10 and 11 (but not the italic heading before paragraph 10).
(6) Before paragraph 12 insert—

"11A—

(1) This paragraph applies to a power to make, confirm or approve subordinate legislation which is conferred—

(a) on or after the day on which this Act is passed, and
(b) before the day on which section 9 of the Retained EU Law (Revocation and Reform) Act 2023 comes into force.

(2) The power is to be read, so far as the context permits or requires, as being capable of being exercised to modify (or, as the case may be, result in the modification of) any retained direct EU legislation or anything which is retained EU law by virtue of section 4.
(3) But sub-paragraph (2) enables a power in retained direct minor EU legislation to be exercised to modify (or result in the modification of) any retained direct principal EU legislation or anything which is retained EU law by virtue of section 4 only if—

(a) the modification is—

(i) consistent with any retained direct principal EU legislation or anything which is retained EU law by virtue of section 4, and
(ii) supplementary, incidental or consequential in connection with any modification of any retained direct minor EU legislation, or

(b) the power is a power to make, confirm or approve transitional, transitory or saving provision.

11B—

(1) This paragraph applies to a power to make, confirm or approve subordinate legislation which is conferred on or after the day on which section 9 of the Retained EU Law (Revocation and Reform) Act 2023 comes into force.
(2) The power is to be read, so far as applicable and unless the contrary intention appears, as being capable of being exercised to modify (or, as the case may be, result in the modification of) any retained direct EU legislation or anything which is retained EU law by virtue of section 4.
(3) But sub-paragraph (2) enables a power in retained direct minor EU legislation to be exercised to modify (or result in the modification

of) any retained direct principal EU legislation or anything which is retained EU law by virtue of section 4 only if—

(a) the modification is—

(i) consistent with any retained direct principal EU legislation or anything which is retained EU law by virtue of section 4, and
(ii) supplementary, incidental or consequential in connection with any modification of any retained direct minor EU legislation, or

(b) the power is a power to make, confirm or approve transitional, transitory or saving provision.

(4) For the purposes of sub-paragraph (2), there is no contrary intention merely because a power is expressed as being capable of being exercised—

(a) to modify all enactments or a particular category of enactments, or
(b) to make a particular category of modifications to all enactments or to a particular category of enactments."

(7) In paragraph 12—

(a) in sub-paragraphs (1) and (2) for "10 and 11" substitute "11A and 11B";
(b) after sub-paragraph (3) insert—

"(4) Sub-paragraph (5) applies in relation to a power if—

(a) paragraph 11A applies in relation to the power, and
(b) immediately before the coming into force of section 9 of the Retained EU Law (Revocation and Reform) Act 2023, and by virtue of a combination of provision in the power and paragraph 10 or 11 as it then had effect, the power was capable of being exercised to modify (or, as the case may be, result in the modification of) any retained direct EU legislation or anything which is retained EU law by virtue of section 4.

(5) The continued existence of the provision in the power does not prevent the context from permitting or requiring the power to be read in accordance with paragraph 11A so far as the reading provided for by that paragraph is not provided for by the provision concerned (and, accordingly, the power continues to be

capable of being exercised as mentioned in sub-paragraph (4) on and after the coming into force of section 9 of the Retained EU Law (Revocation and Reform) Act 2023)."

(8) Part 1 of Schedule 3 contains amendments altering the parliamentary procedure applicable to certain powers when they modify retained direct EU legislation.

(9) Part 2 of that Schedule contains amendments consequential on the amendments made by this section.

10 Procedural requirements

(1) In Schedule 8 to the European Union (Withdrawal) Act 2018 omit—

(a) paragraph 13 (affirmative procedure for instruments which amend or revoke subordinate legislation made under section 2(2) of the European Communities Act 1972);

(b) paragraph 14 (enhanced scrutiny procedure for instruments which amend or revoke subordinate legislation made under section 2(2) the European Communities Act 1972);

(c) paragraph 15 (explanatory statements for instruments which amend or revoke subordinate legislation made under section 2(2) of that Act);

including the italic headings before paragraphs 13 and 14 (but not the italic heading before paragraph 15).

(2) In consequence of the amendments made by subsection (1)—

(a) in section 7(5) of the European Union (Withdrawal) Act 2018 for paragraph (d) substitute—

"(d) paragraph 16 of Schedule 8 (information about Scottish instruments which amend or revoke subordinate legislation under section 2(2) of the European Communities Act 1972),";

(b) in paragraph 16 of Schedule 8 to that Act, for sub-paragraph (7) substitute—

"(7) The references in this paragraph to subordinate legislation made under section 2(2) of the European Communities Act 1972—

(a) do not include references to any provision of such legislation which is made (whether or not by way of amendment) otherwise than under section 2(2) of that Act, and

(b) do include references to subordinate legislation made otherwise than under section 2(2) of that Act so far as that legislation is amended by provision made under that section (but do not include references to any primary legislation so far as so amended).";

(c) in Schedule 5 to the European Union (Withdrawal Agreement) Act 2020 omit paragraph 54(8) to (10).

(3) The amendments made by this section—

(a) so far as relating to paragraph 13 of Schedule 8 to the European Union (Withdrawal) Act 2018, do not apply to any statutory instrument where a draft of the instrument has been laid before each House of Parliament (or, as the case may be, the House of Commons only) before the day on which this Act is passed;
(b) so far as relating to paragraph 14 of that Schedule, do not apply to any statutory instrument or draft statutory instrument where a draft of the instrument has been published under sub-paragraph (2) of that paragraph before the day on which this Act is passed;
(c) so far as relating to paragraph 15 of that Schedule, do not apply to any statutory instrument or draft statutory instrument where—

(i) a statement has been made under sub-paragraph (2) or (3) of that paragraph before the day on which this Act is passed, or
(ii) the instrument or draft has been laid before each House of Parliament (or, as the case may be, the House of Commons only) before the day on which this Act is passed and no statement has been made under sub-paragraph (2) or (3) of that paragraph.

Powers relating to retained EU law and assimilated law

11 Power to restate retained EU law

(1) A relevant national authority may by regulations restate, to any extent, any secondary retained EU law.
(2) In this Act "secondary retained EU law" means—

(a) any retained EU law that is not primary legislation;
(b) any retained EU law that is primary legislation the text of which was inserted by subordinate legislation.

(3) A restatement is not retained EU law.
(4) Any effect which is produced in relation to the thing being restated by virtue of the retained EU law mentioned in subsection (5) does not apply in relation to the restatement.
(5) The retained EU law referred to in subsection (4) is—

(a) the principle of the supremacy of EU law,
(b) retained general principles of EU law, and
(c) anything which is retained EU law by virtue of section 4 or 6(3) or (6) of the European Union (Withdrawal) Act 2018.

(6) But a restatement may, if the relevant authority considers it appropriate, itself produce an effect that is equivalent to an effect referred to in subsection (4).
(7) No regulations may be made under this section after the end of 2023.
(8) In this section—

"restatement": references to restatement, in relation to anything which is retained EU law by virtue of section 4 or 6(3) or (6) of the European Union (Withdrawal) Act 2018, include codification;
"retained general principles of EU law" has the meaning given by section 6(7) of the European Union (Withdrawal) Act 2018.

12 Power to restate assimilated law or reproduce sunsetted retained EU rights, powers, liabilities etc.

(1) A relevant national authority may by regulations restate, to any extent, any secondary assimilated law.
(2) In this Act "secondary assimilated law" means—

(a) any assimilated law that is not primary legislation;
(b) any assimilated law that is primary legislation the text of which was inserted by subordinate legislation.

(3) A restatement is not assimilated law.
(4) Any effect which is produced in relation to the thing being restated by virtue of anything that is assimilated law by virtue of section 6(3) or (6) of the European Union (Withdrawal) Act 2018 does not apply in relation to the restatement.
(5) But a restatement may, if the relevant national authority considers it appropriate, itself produce an effect that is equivalent to an effect referred to in subsection (4).
(6) A restatement may also, if the relevant national authority considers it appropriate, produce an effect that is equivalent to an effect within subsection (7).
(7) An effect is within this subsection if it would, but for sections 2 to 4, be produced in relation to the thing being restated by virtue of—

(a) the principle of the supremacy of EU law,
(b) retained general principles of EU law, or
(c) anything which was retained EU law by virtue of section 4 of the European Union (Withdrawal) Act 2018.

(8) A relevant national authority may by regulations reproduce, to any extent, the effect that anything which was retained EU law by virtue of section 4 or 6(3) or (6) of European Union (Withdrawal) Act 2018 would have, but for sections 2 to 4 of this Act.

(9) No regulations may be made under this section after 23 June 2026.

(10) In this section—

"restatement": references to restatement, in relation to anything which is assimilated law by virtue of section 6(3) or (6) of the European Union (Withdrawal) Act 2018, include codification;

"retained general principles of EU law" has the meaning that was given by section 6(7) of the European Union (Withdrawal) Act 2018 immediately before the end of 2023.

13 Powers to restate or reproduce: general

(1) This section applies for the purposes of sections 11 and 12.

(2) A restatement may use words or concepts that are different from those used in the law being restated.

(3) A restatement may make any change which the relevant national authority considers appropriate for one or more of the following purposes—

(a) resolving ambiguities;
(b) removing doubts or anomalies;
(c) facilitating improvement in the clarity or accessibility of the law (including by omitting anything which is legally unnecessary).

(4) Regulations under section 11 or 12—

(a) may make provision about the relationship between what is restated and a relevant enactment specified in the regulations, but
(b) subject to that, may not make express provision about the relationship between what is restated and other enactments.

(5) Regulations under section 11 or 12 may not codify or reproduce the principle of the supremacy of EU law or a retained general principle of EU law.

(6) Nothing in subsection (5)—

(a) prevents regulations under section 11 or 12 from codifying or reproducing, in relation to a particular enactment, an effect equivalent to an effect which is produced, or would but for sections 2 to 4 be produced, in relation to the enactment by virtue of the principle of supremacy of EU law or retained general principles of EU law, or
(b) prevents regulations under section 11 or 12 which codify or reproduce anything which is or was retained EU law by virtue of section

4 of the European Union (Withdrawal) Act 2018 from producing an effect equivalent to an effect which is produced, or would but for sections 2 to 4 be produced, in relation to that thing by virtue of the principle of supremacy of EU law or retained general principles of EU law.

(7) The provision that may be made by regulations under section 11 or 12 may be made by modifying any enactment.

(8) In sections 11 and 12, references to producing an effect that is equivalent to another effect are to doing so by express provision or otherwise.

(9) In subsection (4)(a) "relevant enactment" means—

- (a) if the provision made by the regulations is made by modifying assimilated direct EU legislation, any assimilated direct EU legislation;
- (b) otherwise, any domestic enactment (as defined by section 5 of the European Union (Withdrawal) Act 2018).

(10) In subsections (5) and (6) "retained general principles of EU law" has the same meaning as in section 11 or 12 (as the case may be).

(11) In this section "restatement"—

- (a) in relation to section 11, has the same meaning as in that section;
- (b) in relation to section 12, has the same meaning as in that section but also includes reproduction;

and similar references are to be read accordingly.

14 Powers to revoke or replace

(1) A relevant national authority may by regulations revoke any secondary retained EU law without replacing it.

(2) A relevant national authority may by regulations revoke any secondary retained EU law and replace it with such provision as the relevant national authority considers to be appropriate and to achieve the same or similar objectives.

(3) A relevant national authority may by regulations revoke any secondary retained EU law and make such alternative provision as the relevant national authority considers appropriate.

(4) Regulations under subsection (2) or (3)—

- (a) may confer a power to make subordinate legislation that corresponds or is similar to a power to make subordinate legislation conferred by secondary retained EU law revoked by the regulations (and may not otherwise confer a power to make subordinate legislation);
- (b) subject to that, may confer functions (including discretions) on any person;

(c) may create a criminal offence that corresponds or is similar to a criminal offence created by secondary retained EU law revoked by the regulations (and may not otherwise create a criminal offence);
(d) may provide for the imposition of monetary penalties in cases that correspond or are similar to cases in which secondary retained EU law revoked by the regulations enables monetary penalties to be imposed (and may not otherwise provide for the imposition of monetary penalties);
(e) may provide for the charging of fees;
(f) may not—

(i) impose taxation;
(ii) establish a public authority.

(5) No provision may be made by a relevant national authority under this section in relation to a particular subject area unless the relevant national authority considers that the overall effect of the changes made by it under this section (including changes made previously) in relation to that subject area does not increase the regulatory burden.
(6) For the purposes of subsection (5), the creation of a voluntary scheme is not to be regarded as increasing the regulatory burden.
(7) The provision that may be made by regulations under this section may be made by modifying any secondary retained EU law.
(8) Any provision made by virtue of this section is not retained EU law.
(9) No regulations may be made under this section after 23 June 2026.
(10) In this section—

"burden" includes (among other things)—

(a) a financial cost;
(b) an administrative inconvenience;
(c) an obstacle to trade or innovation;
(d) an obstacle to efficiency, productivity or profitability;
(e) a sanction (criminal or otherwise) which affects the carrying on of any lawful activity;

"revoke"—

(a) includes repeal, and
(b) in relation to anything which is retained EU law by virtue of section 4 of the European Union (Withdrawal) Act 2018, means provide that it is not recognised or available in domestic law (and, accordingly, not to be enforced, allowed or followed);

"secondary retained EU law": references to secondary retained EU law are to be read after the end of 2023 as references to secondary assimilated law.

(11) In subsection (8) the reference to retained EU law is to be read after the end of 2023 as a reference to assimilated law.

15 Power to update

(1) A relevant national authority may by regulations make such modifications of any secondary retained EU law, or of any provision made by virtue of section 11, 12 or 14, as the relevant national authority considers appropriate to take account of—

(a) changes in technology, or
(b) developments in scientific understanding.

(2) In subsection (1), the reference to secondary retained EU law is to be read after the end of 2023 as a reference to secondary assimilated law.

16 Power to remove or reduce burdens

(1) Part 1 of the Legislative and Regulatory Reform Act 2006 (order-making powers) is amended as follows.
(2) In section 1(6) (power to remove or reduce burdens: definition of "legislation") after paragraph (aa) (and before the "or" at the end of the paragraph) insert—

"(ab) any retained direct EU legislation,".

(3) In section 12 (procedure: introductory) after subsection (2) insert—

"(3) Paragraph 4 of Schedule 8 to the European Union (Withdrawal) Act 2018 (procedure for certain modifications of retained direct EU legislation or anything which is retained EU law by virtue of section 4 of that Act) does not apply in relation to orders under this Part."

Assimilated EU law dashboard and report

17 Assimilated law dashboard and report

(1) The Secretary of State must within the period of 30 days beginning with the day after the end of each reporting period—

(a) update the assimilated law dashboard;
(b) publish and lay before Parliament a report on the revocation and reform of assimilated law.

(2) The report must—

(a) provide a summary of the data on the assimilated law dashboard (as updated under subsection (1)(a));
(b) set out the progress that has been made in revoking and reforming assimilated law during the reporting period to which the report relates;
(c) set out His Majesty's Government's plans to revoke and reform assimilated law in subsequent reporting periods.

(3) The plans that must be set out under subsection (2)(c) must include a list of the provisions of assimilated law which His Majesty's Government intends to revoke or reform.
(4) The reporting periods are—

(a) the period beginning with the day on which this Act is passed and ending with 23 December 2023;
(b) each subsequent period of 6 months, subject to subsection (5).

(5) The last reporting period ends with 23 June 2026.
(6) If the Secretary of State does not meet the requirements in subsection (1) in relation to a reporting period, the Secretary of State must—

(a) explain why in a statement made in writing, and
(b) publish the statement and lay it before Parliament.

(7) In this section—

"assimilated law dashboard" means the database on assimilated law maintained and made publicly available by the Secretary of State;
"revoke" has the same meaning as in section 14.

(8) In subsection (2), "reform" includes "replace".
(9) In relation to the report under subsection (1)(b) in respect of the period ending with 23 June 2026, ignore subsection (2)(c).

Business impact target

18 Abolition of business impact target

(1) In the Small Business, Enterprise and Employment Act 2015, omit sections 21 to 27 (business impact target) including the italic heading before section 21.
(2) In consequence of subsection (1), that Act is amended as specified in subsections (3) and (4).

(3) In section 29(5) (definition of "voluntary or community body") for "has the meaning given in section 27." substitute "means any of the following—

(a) a trade union (within the meaning of section 1 of the Trade Union and Labour Relations (Consolidation) Act 1992 or Article 3 of the Industrial Relations (Northern Ireland) Order 1992 (S.I. 1992/807 (N.I. 5)));
(b) an unincorporated body which does not distribute any surplus it makes to its members;
(c) a charity;
(d) a company limited by guarantee which does not distribute any surplus it makes to its members;
(e) a registered society within the meaning given by section 1 of the Co-operative and Community Benefit Societies Act 2014;
(f) a registered society within the meaning given by section 1A of the Co-operative and Community Benefit Societies Act (Northern Ireland) 1969 (c. 24 (N.I.)) or a credit union within the meaning of the Credit Unions (Northern Ireland) Order 1985 (S.I. 1985/1205 (N.I. 12));
(g) a community interest company;
(h) a charitable incorporated organisation within the meaning of Part 11 of the Charities Act 2011 or of the Charities Act (Northern Ireland) 2008 (c. 12 (N.I.));
(i) a Scottish charitable incorporated organisation within the meaning of Chapter 7 of Part 1 of the Charities and Trustee Investment (Scotland) Act 2005 (asp 10)."

(4) In section 33(6), in paragraph (b) of the definition of "undertaking" for "section 27" substitute "section 29(5)".
(5) In consequence of subsection (1), also omit the following—

(a) in the Enterprise Act 2016, section 14 (and the italic heading before it) and Schedule 2;
(b) in Schedule 6 to the Wales Act 2017, paragraph 107;
(c) in Schedule 3 to the Advanced Research and Invention Agency Act 2022, paragraphs 9 and 10;
(d) in the Schedule to the Dissolution and Calling of Parliament Act 2022, paragraphs 27 to 31 (including the italic heading before paragraph 27).

Final provisions

19 Consequential provision

(1) A relevant national authority may by regulations make such provision as the relevant national authority considers appropriate in consequence of this Act.

(2) The provision referred to in subsection (1) includes provision modifying any enactment, including this Act.

20 Regulations: general

(1) A power to make regulations under this Act includes power to make—

(a) different provision for different purposes or areas;
(b) supplementary, incidental, consequential, transitional, transitory or saving provision (including provision modifying any enactment, including this Act).

(2) Schedule 4 contains restrictions on the powers of devolved authorities to make regulations under this Act.
(3) Schedule 5 contains provision about the procedure for making regulations under this Act.
(4) A prohibition in this Act on making regulations after any particular time does not affect the continuation in force of regulations made before that time.
(5) Section 28 of the Small Business, Enterprise and Employment Act 2015 (duty to review regulatory provisions in secondary legislation) does not apply in relation to any power to make regulations under this Act.

21 Interpretation

(1) In this Act—
"assimilated law" has the meaning given by section 5(1);
"devolved authority" means—

(a) the Scottish Ministers,
(b) the Welsh Ministers, or
(c) a Northern Ireland department;

"domestic law" means the law of England and Wales, Scotland or Northern Ireland;
"enactment" means—

(a) an enactment (whenever passed or made) contained in, or in an instrument made under, any primary legislation, or
(b) any assimilated direct legislation;

"Minister of the Crown" has the same meaning as in the Ministers of the Crown Act 1975 and also includes the Commissioners for His Majesty's Revenue and Customs;
"modify" includes amend, repeal or revoke (and related expressions are to be read accordingly);

"Northern Ireland devolved authority" means—

(a) the First Minister and deputy First Minister acting jointly,
(b) a Northern Ireland Minister, or
(c) a Northern Ireland department;

"primary legislation" means—

(a) an Act of Parliament,
(b) an Act of the Scottish Parliament,
(c) an Act or Measure of Senedd Cymru, or
(d) Northern Ireland legislation;

"relevant national authority" means—

(a) a Minister of the Crown,
(b) a devolved authority, or
(c) a Minister of the Crown acting jointly with one or more devolved authorities;

"secondary assimilated law" has the meaning given by section 12(2);
"secondary retained EU law" has the meaning given by section 11(2);
"subordinate legislation" means—

(a) an instrument (other than an instrument that is Northern Ireland legislation) made under any primary legislation, or
(b) an instrument made on or after IP completion day under any assimilated direct legislation.

(2) In this Act—
(a) references to an instrument made under an Act include in particular any Order in Council, order, rules, regulations, scheme, warrant or byelaw made under an Act;
(b) references to an instrument made under any assimilated direct legislation include in particular any Order in Council, order, rules, regulations, scheme, warrant or byelaw made under any assimilated direct legislation.
(3) In this Act references to anything which is retained EU law by virtue of section 4 of the European Union (Withdrawal) Act 2018 include references to any modifications, made on or after IP completion day, of the rights, powers, liabilities, obligations, restrictions, remedies or procedures concerned.

22 *Commencement, transitional and savings*

(1) The following provisions come into force on the day on which this Act is passed—

(a) sections 1 and 2;
(b) section 5(1), (2) and (4) to (7);
(c) section 7;
(d) sections 9 to 17 and Schedule 3;
(e) sections 19 to 21, this section, section 23 and Schedules 4 and 5.

(2) Section 18 comes into force at the end of the period of two months beginning with the day on which this Act is passed.
(3) The other provisions of this Act come into force on such day as a Minister of the Crown may by regulations appoint.
(4) A relevant national authority may by regulations make such transitional, transitory or saving provision as the relevant national authority considers appropriate in connection with—

(a) the coming into force of any provision of this Act,
(b) the revocation of anything by section 1, or
(c) anything ceasing to be recognised or available in domestic law (and, accordingly, ceasing to be enforced, allowed or followed) as a result of section 2.

(5) Sections 2, 3 and 4 do not apply in relation to anything occurring before the end of 2023.
(6) The amendments made by Schedule 2 do not apply as regards any time at or before the end of 2023.

23 *Extent and short title*

(1) Subject to subsection (2), this Act extends to England and Wales, Scotland and Northern Ireland.
(2) Any amendment, repeal or revocation made by this Act has the same extent within the United Kingdom as the provision to which it relates.
(3) This Act may be cited as the Retained EU Law (Revocation and Reform) Act 2023.

Schedules 1 to 4

[Omitted]

6 Arbitration Act 2025

Applicable law

1 Law applicable to arbitration agreement

(1) The Arbitration Act 1996 is amended as follows.
(2) After section 6 insert—

"6A Law applicable to arbitration agreement

(1) The law applicable to an arbitration agreement is—

(a) the law that the parties expressly agree applies to the arbitration agreement, or
(b) where no such agreement is made, the law of the seat of the arbitration in question.

(2) For the purposes of subsection (1), agreement between the parties that a particular law applies to an agreement of which the arbitration agreement forms a part does not constitute express agreement that that law also applies to the arbitration agreement.
(3) Subsection (1) does not apply to an arbitration agreement derived from a standing offer to submit disputes to arbitration where the offer is contained in—

(a) a treaty, or
(b) legislation of a country or territory outside the United Kingdom.

(4) In this section—

"legislation" includes any provision of a legislative character;
"treaty" includes any international agreement (and any protocol or annex to a treaty or international agreement)."

DOI: 10.4324/9781003673194-7

(3) In section 2 (scope of application of provisions), in subsection (2) after the opening words insert—

"(za) section 6A (law applicable to arbitration agreement),".

The arbitral tribunal

2 Impartiality: duty of disclosure

(1) The Arbitration Act 1996 is amended as follows.
(2) After section 23 insert—

"23A Impartiality: duty of disclosure

An individual who has been approached by a person in connection with the individual's possible appointment as an arbitrator must, as soon as reasonably practical, disclose to the person any relevant circumstances of which the individual is, or becomes, aware.
An arbitrator must, as soon as reasonably practical, disclose to the parties to the arbitral proceedings any relevant circumstances of which the arbitrator is, or becomes, aware.
For the purposes of this section—

(a) "relevant circumstances", in relation to an individual, are circumstances that might reasonably give rise to justifiable doubts as to the individual's impartiality in relation to the proceedings, or potential proceedings, concerned, and
(b) an individual is to be treated as being aware of circumstances of which the individual ought reasonably to be aware."

(3) In Schedule 1 (mandatory provisions), after the entry for section 13, insert—

"section 23A (impartiality: duty of disclosure);".

3 Immunity of arbitrator: application for removal

(1) The Arbitration Act 1996 is amended as follows.
(2) In section 24 (power of court to remove arbitrator), after subsection (5) insert—

"(5A) The court may not order the arbitrator to pay costs in proceedings under this section unless any act or omission of the arbitrator in connection with the
proceedings is shown to have been in bad faith."

(3) In section 29(1) (general immunity of arbitrator), at the end insert "(and see section 24(5A) (immunity in respect of costs of proceedings for removal))".

4 Immunity of arbitrator: resignation

(1) The Arbitration Act 1996 is amended as follows.

(2) In section 25 (resignation of arbitrator)—

(a) in subsection (1), omit paragraph (b) (together with the "and" before it);

(b) for subsections (3) and (4) substitute—

"(3) Where an arbitrator resigns, a relevant person may (upon notice to the other relevant persons) apply to the court to make such order as it thinks fit with respect to the arbitrator's entitlement (if any) to feesor expenses or the repayment of any fees or expenses already paid.

(4) For the purposes of subsection (3), each of the parties and the arbitrator is a "relevant person".";

(c) in the heading, at the end insert ": entitlement to fees or expenses".

(3) In section 29 (immunity of arbitrator)—

(a) omit subsection (3);

(b) at the end insert—

"(4) An arbitrator's resignation does not give rise to any liability for the arbitrator unless it is shown that the resignation was, in all the circumstances, unreasonable.

(5) But subsection (4) is subject to—

(a) agreement reached between the parties and the arbitrator as mentioned in section 25(1)(a);

(b) an order made under section 25(3).

(4) In the following provisions, for "25(3)(b)" substitute "25(3)"—

(a) section 28(4) (joint and several liability of parties to arbitrators for fees and expenses);

(b) section 64(3) (recoverable fees and expenses of arbitrators);

(c) paragraphs 3(2) and 10(2) of Schedule 2 (modifications in relation to judge-arbitrators).

Jurisdiction of tribunal

5 Court determination of jurisdiction of tribunal

In section 32 of the Arbitration Act 1996 (determination of preliminary point of jurisdiction), after subsection (1) insert—

"(1A) An application under this section must not be considered to the extent that it is in respect of a question on which the tribunal has already ruled."

6 Power to award costs despite no substantive jurisdiction

(1) Section 61 of the Arbitration Act 1996 (award of costs) is amended as follows.

(2) In subsection (1), omit ", subject to any agreement of the parties".

(3) After subsection (1) insert—

"(1A) It is irrelevant for the purposes of subsection (1) whether the tribunal has ruled, or a court has held, that the tribunal has no substantive jurisdiction or has exceeded its substantive jurisdiction."

(4) In subsection (2), omit "Unless the parties otherwise agree,".

(5) After subsection (2) insert—

"(3) Subsections (1), (1A) and (2) are subject to any agreement of the parties."

Arbitral proceedings and powers of the court

7 Power to make award on summary basis

After section 39 of the Arbitration Act 1996 insert—

"39A Power to make award on summary basis

(1) Unless the parties otherwise agree, the arbitral tribunal may, on an application made by a party to the proceedings (upon notice to the other parties), make an award on a summary basis in relation to a claim, or a particular issue arising in a claim, if the tribunal considers that—

(a) a party has no real prospect of succeeding on the claim or issue, or

(b) a party has no real prospect of succeeding in the defence of the claim or issue.

(2) For the purposes of subsection (1), an arbitral tribunal makes an award "on a summary basis" in relation to a claim or issue if the tribunal has exercised its power under section 34(1) (to decide all procedural and evidential matters) with a view to expediting the proceedings on the claim or issue.

(3) Before exercising its power under section 34(1) as mentioned in subsection (2), an arbitral tribunal must afford the parties a reasonable opportunity to make representations to the tribunal."

8 Emergency arbitrators

(1) The Arbitration Act 1996 is amended as follows.

(2) After section 41 insert—

"41A Emergency arbitrators

(1) This section applies where—

(a) the parties have agreed to the application of rules that provide for the appointment of an individual as an emergency arbitrator, and

(b) an emergency arbitrator has been appointed pursuant to those rules.

(2) Unless otherwise agreed by the parties, if without showing sufficient cause a party fails to comply with any order or directions of the emergency arbitrator, the emergency arbitrator may make a peremptory order to the same effect, prescribing such time for compliance with it as the emergency arbitrator considers appropriate."

(3) In section 41(7) (peremptory orders of tribunal), in the opening words—

(a) after "peremptory order" insert "of the tribunal";

(b) omit "tribunal's"

(4) In section 42 (enforcement of peremptory orders of tribunal)—

(a) in subsection (1), at the end insert "or (as the case may be) the emergency arbitrator";

(b) in subsection (2)(a) and (b), after "the tribunal" insert "or the emergency arbitrator";

(c) in subsection (3), for "tribunal's order" substitute "peremptory order";

(d) in subsection (4), for "tribunal's order" substitute "peremptory order";

(e) in the heading, at the end insert "or emergency arbitrator".

(5) In section 44 (court powers exercisable in support of arbitral proceedings)—

(a) for subsection (4) substitute—

"(4) If the case is not one of urgency, the court may act only on the application of a party to the arbitral proceedings made with—

(a) the permission of the tribunal or (as the case may be) the emergency arbitrator, or

(b) the agreement in writing of the other parties.

(4A) An application under subsection (4) may be made only upon notice to the other parties and to the tribunal or the emergency arbitrator.";

(b) in subsection (5), after "tribunal" insert "or the emergency arbitrator";

(c) in subsection (6), after "tribunal" insert ", the emergency arbitrator".

(6) In section 82(1) (minor definitions)—

(a) after the definition of "dispute" insert—

"“emergency arbitrator” means an individual appointed as mentioned in section 41A(1);";

(b) in the definition of "peremptory order", after "section 41(5)" insert "or 41A(2),".

(7) In section 83 (index of defined expressions), after the entry for "dispute" insert—

"emergency arbitrator section 82(1) (and see section 41A(1))".

9 Court powers exercisable in support of arbitral proceedings in respect of third parties

(1) Section 44 of the Arbitration Act 1996 (court powers exercisable in support of arbitral proceedings) is amended as follows.

(2) In subsection (1), after "making orders" insert "(whether in relation to a party or any other person)".

(3) For subsection (7) substitute—

"(6A) Subject to subsection (7), an appeal lies from a decision of the court under this section.

(7) The leave of the court is required for any such appeal by a party or proposed party to the arbitral proceedings."

Powers of the court in relation to award

10 Challenging the award: remedies available to the court

(1) Section 67 of the Arbitration Act 1996 (challenging the award: substantive jurisdiction) is amended as follows.

(2) In subsection (1), for paragraph (b) substitute—

"(b) challenging an award made by the tribunal on the merits because the tribunal did not have substantive jurisdiction."

(3) For subsection (3) substitute—

"(3) On an application under this section, the court may by order—

(a) confirm the award,
(b) vary the award,
(c) remit the award to the tribunal, in whole or in part, for reconsideration,
(d) set aside the award, in whole or in part, or
(e) declare the award to be of no effect, in whole or in part.

(3A) The court must not exercise its power to set aside or to declare an award to be of no effect, in whole or in part, unless it is satisfied that it would be inappropriate to remit the matters in question to the tribunal for reconsideration."

11 Procedure on challenge under section 67 of the Arbitration Act 1996

In section 67 of the Arbitration Act 1996 (challenging the award: substantive jurisdiction), after subsection (3A) (as inserted by section 10(3)) insert—

"(3B) Rules of court about the procedure to be followed on an application under this section may, in particular, include provision within subsection (3C) in relation to a case where the application—

(a) relates to an objection as to the arbitral tribunal's substantive jurisdiction on which the tribunal has already ruled, and
(b) is made by a party that took part in the arbitral proceedings.

(3C) Provision is within this subsection if it provides that subject to the court ruling otherwise in the interests of justice—

(a) a ground for the objection that was not raised before the arbitral tribunal must not be raised before the court unless the applicant shows that, at the time the applicant took part in the proceedings, the applicant did not know and could not with reasonable diligence have discovered the ground;

(b) evidence that was not put before the tribunal must not be considered by the court unless the applicant shows that, at the time the applicant took part in the proceedings, the applicant could not with reasonable diligence have put the evidence before the tribunal;

(c) evidence that was heard by the tribunal must not be re-heard by the court.

(3D) Subsection (3B) does not limit the generality of the power to make rules of court."

12 Challenging the award: time limit

(1) Section 70 of the Arbitration Act 1996 (challenge or appeal: supplementary provisions) is amended as follows.

(2) In subsection (3), for the words from "the date of the award" to the end substitute "the applicable date".

(3) After subsection (3) insert—

"(3A) In subsection (3), "the applicable date" means—

(a) in a case where there has been any arbitral process of appeal or review, the date when the applicant or appellant was notified of the result of that process;

(b) in a case where the tribunal has, under section 57, made a material correction to an award or has made a material additional award, the date of the correction or additional award;

(c) in a case where a material application for a correction to an award or for an additional award has been made to the tribunal under section 57 and the tribunal has decided not to grant the application, the date when the applicant or appellant was notified of that decision;

(d) in any other case, the date of the award.

(3B) For the purposes of subsection (3A)—

(a) a correction to an award,

(b) an additional award, or

(c) an application under section 57, is "material" if any matter to which it relates is material to the application or appeal under section 67, 68 or 69."

(4) At the end insert—

"(9) In this section, a reference to available recourse, or to anything done, under section 57 includes a reference to available recourse, or to anything equivalent done, pursuant to agreement reached between the parties as mentioned in section 57(1)."

Appeals from High Court decisions

13 Appeals to Court of Appeal from High Court decisions

(1) In section 18(1) of the Senior Courts Act 1981 (restrictions on appeals to Court of Appeal), for paragraph (g) substitute—

"(g) from a decision of the High Court under Part 1 of the Arbitration Act 1996 in a case where that Part makes provision about appeals from the decision, except in accordance with that provision;".

(2) In section 35(2) of the Judicature (Northern Ireland) Act 1978 (appeals to Court of Appeal from High Court), for paragraph (fa) substitute—

"(fa) from a decision of the High Court under Part 1 of the Arbitration Act 1996 in a case where that Part makes provision about appeals from the decision, except in accordance with that provision;".

(3) In Schedule 3 to the Arbitration Act 1996 (consequential amendments), omit paragraphs 34(2) and 37(2).

Miscellaneous minor amendments

14 Requirements to be met for court to consider applications

(1) The Arbitration Act 1996 is amended as follows.

(2) In section 32 (determination by court of preliminary point of jurisdiction)—

(a) in subsection (2)(b), omit the words from "and the court" to the end;
(b) omit subsection (3);
(c) in subsection (5), for "the conditions specified in subsection (2) are" substitute "either condition specified in subsection (2) is".

(3) In section 45 (determination by court of preliminary point of law)—

(a) in subsection (2)(b), omit the words from "and the court" to the end;
(b) in subsection (3), omit the words from "and, unless" to the end;
(c) in subsection (5), for "the conditions specified in subsection (2) are" substitute "either condition specified in subsection (2) is".

15 Repeal of provisions relating to domestic arbitration agreements

Omit the following provisions of the Arbitration Act 1996—

(a) sections 85 to 87 (domestic arbitration agreements) (which are not in force),together with the italic heading before section 85, and

(b) section 88 (power to repeal or amend sections 85 to 87).

Final provisions

Sections 16–18 [Omitted]

Section II

Statutory Instruments

7 Civil Jurisdiction and Judgments (Amendment) (EU Exit) Regulations 2019

Part 1

Introduction

Citation, commencement and extent

1. — (1) These Regulations may be cited as the Civil Jurisdiction and Judgments (Amendment) (EU Exit) Regulations 2019 and come into force on exit day.

(2) Subject to paragraph (3), these Regulations extend to England and Wales, Scotland and Northern Ireland.

(3) Any amendment made by these Regulations has the same extent as the provision it amends.

Part 2

Amendment of primary legislation

Administration of Justice Act 1970

2. [Omitted]

Attachment of Earnings Act 1971

3. [Omitted]

Civil Jurisdiction and Judgments Act 1982

4. The Civil Jurisdiction and Judgments Act 1982(**b**) is amended as follows.

5. … [Reg 5 omitted]

6. — (1) Section 1 (interpretation of references to the Brussels and other Conventions and Contracting States) is amended as follows.

(2) In subsection (1)—

DOI: 10.4324/9781003673194-9

(a) omit the definitions of—
(i) "the 1996 Accession Convention";
(ii) "the Brussels Conventions";
(iii) "the Lugano Convention";

(b) in the definition of "the Regulation"—
(i) omit "as amended from time to time and"; and
(ii) after "p4)", insert "as that Regulation had effect and was applied immediately before IP completion day".

(3) Omit subsection (2).
(4) In subsection (3)—

(a) in the definition of "Contracting State", omit paragraphs (a) and (b);
(b) omit the definition of "Brussels Contracting State";
(c) omit the definitions of—

(i) "State bound by the Lugano Convention";
(ii) "Regulation State".

(5) Omit subsection (4).

7. Omit section 2 (the Brussels Conventions to have the force of law).
8. Omit section 3 (interpretation of the Brussels Conventions).
9. … [Reg 9 omitted]
10. Omit section 4 (enforcement of judgments, other than maintenance orders, under the 1968 Convention).
11. Omit section 4A (enforcement of judgments, other than maintenance orders, under the Lugano Convention).
12. Omit section 5 (recognition and enforcement of maintenance orders: applications under Article 31 of the 1968 Convention).
13. Omit section 5A (recognition and enforcement of maintenance orders under the Lugano Convention).
14. Omit section 6 (appeals under Articles 37(2) and 41 of the 1968 Convention).
15. Omit section 6A (appeals under Article 44 and Annex IV of the Lugano Convention).
16. —(1) Section 7 (interest on registered judgments) is amended as follows.
(2) In subsection (1)—

(a) omit "Subject to subsection (4),";
(b) omit "4, 4A,";
(c) omit ", 5 or 5A";
(d) omit "apart from section 4(2),".

(2) Omit subsection (3).
(3) Omit subsection (4).
(2) In subsection (5)—

(a) omit "Except as mentioned in subsection (4),";
(b) omit "4, 4A,";
(c) omit ", 5 or 5A".

17. Omit section 8 (currency of payment under registered maintenance orders).

18. —(1) Section 9 (provisions supplementary to Title VII of the 1968 Convention) is amended as follows.

(2) In the heading, for "Provisions supplementary to Title VIII of 1968 Convention" substitute "Provisions supplementary to Article 26 of the 2005 Hague Convention".
(3) In subsection (1)—

(a) omit the words from the beginning to "Lugano Convention and";
(b) for "the Convention in question" substitute "the 2005 Hague Convention".

19. Omit section 10 (allocation within UK of jurisdiction with respect to trusts and consumer contracts where section 16 does not apply).

20. Omit section 11 (proof and admissibility of certain judgments and related documents).

21. Omit section 11A (proof and admissibility of certain judgments and related documents for the purposes of the Lugano Convention).

22. In section 12 (provision for issue of copies of, and certificates in connection with, UK judgments), omit "the 1968 Convention, the Lugano Convention or".

23. Omit section 13 (modifications to cover authentic instruments and court settlements).

24. Omit section 14 (modifications consequential on revision of the Brussels Conventions).

25. —(1) Section 15 (interpretation of Part 1 and consequential amendments) is amended as follows.

(2) In subsection (1)—
(a) in the definition of "judgment", omit the words from "Article 25" to "Lugano Convention or";
(b) omit the definition of "maintenance order";
(c) omit the definition of "payer".

(3) In subsection (2)—

(a) omit "4, 4A,";
(b) omit ", 5 or 5A".

(4) In subsection (3), omit the words from "the 1968" to "Lugano Convention or".

26. Before section 16, insert—

"*Jurisdiction in consumer and employment matters*

Scope of sections 15B to 15E

15A.—(1) Sections 15B to 15E make provision about the jurisdiction of courts in the United Kingdom—

(a) in matters relating to consumer contracts where the consumer is domiciled in the United Kingdom;
(b) in matters relating to individual contracts of employment.

(2) Sections 15B and 15C apply only if the subject-matter of the proceedings and the nature of the proceedings are within the scope of the Regulation as determined by Article 1 of the Regulation (whether or not the Regulation would have had effect before IP completion day in relation to the proceedings).

(3) Sections 15B to 15E do not apply to proceedings of a description listed in Schedule 5 or to proceedings in Scotland under an enactment which confers jurisdiction on a Scottish court in respect of a specific subject-matter on specific grounds.

Jurisdiction in relation to consumer contracts

15B.—(1) This section applies in relation to proceedings whose subject-matter is a matter relating to a consumer contract where the consumer is domiciled in the United Kingdom.

(2) The consumer may bring proceedings against the other party to the consumer contract—

(a) where the other party to the consumer contract is domiciled in the United Kingdom, in the courts of the part of the United Kingdom in which the other party to the consumer contract is domiciled, or
(b) in the courts for the place where the consumer is domiciled (regardless of the domicile of the other party to the consumer contract).

(3) Proceedings may be brought against the consumer by the other party to the consumer contract only in the courts of the part of the United Kingdom in which the consumer is domiciled.

(4) Subsections (2) and (3) are subject to rule 11 of Schedule 4 (and rule 14 of Schedule 4 has effect accordingly).

(5) Subsections (2) and (3) do not affect—

(a) the right (under rule 5(c) of Schedule 4 or otherwise) to bring a counterclaim in the court in which, in accordance with subsection (2) or (3), the original claim is pending,

(b) the operation of rule 3(e) or (h)(ii) of Schedule 4, or

(c) the operation of any other rule of law which permits a person not domiciled in the United Kingdom to be sued in the courts of a part of the United Kingdom.

(6) Subsections (2) and (3) may be departed from only by an agreement—

(a) which is entered into after the dispute has arisen,

(b) which allows the consumer to bring proceedings in courts other than those indicated in this section, or

(c) which is entered into by the consumer and the other party to the contract, both of whom are at the time of conclusion of the contract domiciled or habitually resident in the United Kingdom and in the same part of the United Kingdom, and which confers jurisdiction on the courts of that part of the United Kingdom, provided that such an agreement is not contrary to the law of that part of the United Kingdom.

(7) For the purposes of this section, where a consumer enters into a consumer contract with a party who is not domiciled in the United Kingdom, the other party to the contract is deemed to be domiciled in a particular part of the United Kingdom if that party has a branch, agency or establishment in that part of the United Kingdom and the dispute arose out of the operations of that branch, agency or establishment.

Jurisdiction in relation to individual contracts of employment

15C.— [Omitted]

Further provision as to jurisdiction

15D.— [Omitted]

Interpretation

15E.—(1) In sections 15A to 15D and this section—

"consumer", in relation to a consumer contract, means a person who concludes the contract for a purpose which can be regarded as being outside the person's trade or profession;

"consumer contract" means—

(a) a contract for the sale of goods on instalment credit terms,
(b) a contract for a loan repayable by instalments, or for any other form of credit, made to finance the sale of goods, or
(c) a contract which has been concluded with a person who—

(i) pursues commercial or professional activities in the part of the United Kingdom in which the consumer is domiciled, or
(ii) by any means, directs such activities to that part or to other parts of the United Kingdom including that part,

and which falls within the scope of such activities,

but it does not include a contract of transport other than a contract which, for an inclusive price, provides for a combination of travel and accommodation or a contract of insurance,

"defendant" includes defender.

(2) In determining any question as to the meaning or effect of any provision contained in sections 15A to 15D and this section—

(a) regard is to be had to any relevant principles laid down before IP completion day by the European Court in connection with Title II of the 1968 Convention or Chapter 2 of the Regulation and to any relevant decision of that court before IP completion day as to the meaning or effect of any provision of that Title or Chapter, and
(b) without prejudice to the generality of paragraph (a), the expert reports relating to the 1968 Convention may be considered and are, so far as relevant, to be given such weight as is appropriate in the circumstances."

27. Before section 16, but after the provision inserted by regulation 26, insert— "*Jurisdiction in other civil proceedings*".

28. —(1) Section 16 (allocation within UK of jurisdiction in certain civil proceedings) is amended as follows.

2. In subsection (1)(a), for "has effect" substitute "would have had effect before IP completion day".
3. After subsection (1), insert—

"(1A) This section and Schedule 4 do not apply for the purposes of determining jurisdiction in proceedings in relation to which section 15B, 15C or 15D(2) applies, except as specified in those sections.".

4. In subsection (3)(b), for "the reports mentioned in section 3(3)" substitute "the expert reports relating to the 1968 Convention".
5. After subsection (3) insert—

"(3A) The requirement in subsection (3)(a) applies only in relation to principles laid down, or decisions made, by the European Court before IP completion day.".

6. In subsection (4)—

(a) omit "the Regulation,";
(b) omit "the 1968 Convention, the Lugano Convention";
(c) for "section 17" substitute "sections 15B, 15C, 15D and 17".

29. Before section 18, insert—

"*Recognition of judgments*".

30. In section 18 (enforcement of UK judgments in other parts of the UK), in subsection (7), omit "or section 4 or 5 of this Act".

31. —(1) Section 20 (rules as to jurisdiction in Scotland) is amended as follows.

(2) In subsection (1), omit "the Regulation, to".
(3) In subsection (5)(b), for "the reports mentioned in section 3(3)" substitute "the expert reports relating to the 1968 Convention".
(4) After subsection (5) insert—

"(6) The requirement in subsection (5)(a) applies only in relation to principles laid down, or decisions made, by the European Court before IP completion day."

32. —(1) Section 24 (interim relief and protective measures in cases of doubtful jurisdiction) is amended as follows.

(2) In subsection (1)—

(a) omit paragraph (b), the "or" preceding it, and the "or" following it;
(b) omit paragraph (c) and the "or" following it.

(3) In subsection (2)—

(a) omit paragraph (b), the "or" preceding it, and the "or" following it;
(b) omit paragraph (c) and the "or" following it.

33. —(1) Section 25 (interim relief in England and Wales and Northern Ireland in the absence of substantive proceedings) is amended as follows.

(2) In subsection (1)—

(a) in paragraph (a)—

(i) omit "a Brussels Contracting State or a State bound by the Lugano Convention or";
(ii) omit "or a Regulation State";

(b) in paragraph (b)—

(i) omit "either within the scope of the Regulation, as determined by Article 1 of the Regulation,";
(ii) omit "within scope of the Lugano Convention as determined by Article 1 of the Lugano Convention or";
(iii) omit "the Regulation" in the third place it occurs;
(iv) omit "the Lugano Convention or" in the second place it occurs.

(3) In subsection (3)—

(a) in paragraph (a)—

(i) omit "a Brussels Contracting State or a State bound by the Lugano Convention or";
(ii) omit "or Regulation State";

(b) in paragraph (b)—

(i) omit "the Regulation as determined by Article 1 of the Regulation,";
(iii) omit "the Lugano Convention as determined by Article 1 of the Lugano Convention or".

34. —(1) Section 27 (provisional and protective measures in Scotland in the absence of substantive proceedings) is amended as follows.
(2) In subsection (2)—

(a) in paragraph (a), omit "in another Brussels or Lugano Contracting State, in another Regulation State,";
(b) in paragraph (b), omit "is within the scope of the Regulation as determined by Article 1 of the Regulation,".

(3) In subsection (3)—

(a) in paragraph (a), omit "a Brussels, Lugano Contracting State, Regulation State or";

(b) in paragraph (b), omit "the Regulation as determined by Article 1 of the Regulation or";

(c) in paragraph (d), omit "a Brussels or Lugano Contracting State, Regulation State,".

35 –40. [Omitted]

41. —(1) Section 42 (domicile and seat of corporation or association) is amended as follows.

(2) Omit subsection (2)(a) and the "and" following it.

(3) After subsection (4) insert—

"(4A) For the purposes of sections 15A to 15E and rules 1, 2, 3, 5, 11(a)(ii) and 15(1) in Schedule 4, the requirement in subsection (4) that a corporation or association has its seat in the United Kingdom is to be treated as satisfied if the corporation or association satisfies the requirement in section 42A(2) for having its domicile in the United Kingdom.".

(4) In subsection (6), omit "Subject to subsection (7),".

(5) After subsection (6) insert—

"(6A) Subsections (1), (3) and (6) are subject to section 42A.".

(6) Omit subsection (7).

42. After section 42 insert—

"Domicile of corporation or association for purposes of certain civil proceedings

42A.—(1) This section determines whether a corporation or association is domiciled in the United Kingdom for the purposes of—

(a) sections 15A to 15E, and

(b) section 16(1)(b).

(2) A corporation or association has its domicile in the United Kingdom if and only if—

(a) its registered office is at a place in the United Kingdom,

(b) its place of incorporation is in the United Kingdom (in a case where it has no registered office),

(c) the place under the law of which its formation took place is a place in the United Kingdom (in a case where it has no registered office or place of incorporation),

(d) its central administration is in the United Kingdom, or

(e) its principal place of business is in the United Kingdom.".

43. —(1) Section 43 (seat of corporation or association for the purposes of Article 16(2) of the 1968 Convention and related provisions) is amended as follows.

(2) In the heading, for "Article 16(2) and related" substitute "certain".
(3) Omit subsection (1)(a).
(4) Omit subsection (6).
(5) Omit subsection (7).

44. Omit section 43A (seat of companies or other legal persons, or of associations, for the purposes of Article 22(2) of the Lugano Convention).

45. Omit section 44 (persons deemed to be domiciled in the United Kingdom for certain purposes of the 1968 Convention).

46. Omit section 44A (persons deemed to be domiciled in the United Kingdom for certain purposes of the Lugano Convention).

47 –51. [Omitted]

52. —(1) Section 50 (interpretation: general) is amended as follows.

(2) In the definition of "the Accession Convention" "the 1982 Accession Convention", "the 1989 Accession Convention" and "the 1996 Accession Convention", for ", "the 1989 Accession Convention" and "the 1996 Accession Convention"" substitute "and "the 1989 Accession Convention".

(3) At the appropriate place insert—
""the expert reports relating to the 1968 Convention" means—

(a) the reports by Mr. P. Jenard on the 1968 Convention and the 1971 Protocol;
(b) the report by Professor Peter Schlosser on the Accession Convention;
(c) the report by Professor Demetrios I. Evrigenis and Professor K. D. Kerameus on the 1982 Accession Convention; and
(d) the report by Mr. Martinho de Almeida Cruz, Mr. Manuel Desantes Real and Mr. P. Jenard on the 1989 Accession Convention;".

(4) Omit the definitions of—

(a) "Article";
(b) "Brussels Contracting State";
(c) "the Brussels Conventions";
(d) "the Lugano Convention";
(e) "Regulation State";
(f) "State bound by the Lugano Convention".

(5) In the definition of "tribunal", omit paragraph (b).

53–69. [Omitted]

Part 3

Amendment of subordinate legislation

70–81. [Omitted] **The High Court and County Courts Jurisdiction Order 1991**

Part 4

Treaty rights and obligations

82. [Omitted]

Part 5

Revocation of retained direct EU legislation

83–88. [Omitted]

Regulation (EU) No 1215/2012

89. Regulation (EU) No 1215/2012 of the European Parliament and of the Council of 12 December 2012 on jurisdiction and the recognition and enforcement of judgments in civil and commercial matters (recast) is revoked.

Regulation (EU) No 542/2014

90. Regulation (EU) No 542/2014 of the European Parliament and of the Council of 15 May 2014 amending Regulation (EU) No 1215/2012 as regards the rules to be applied with respect to the Unified Patent Court and the Benelux Court of Justice is revoked.

91. [Omitted]

Part 6

Savings

Savings relating to jurisdiction, recognition and enforcement

92. —(1) Subject to paragraph (5) and to regulation 93, this regulation applies—

(a) where one of the relevant instruments applies immediately before IP completion day to determine questions relating to the jurisdiction of a court in any part of the United Kingdom to hear proceedings of which that court was seised before IP completion day and which are not concluded before IP completion day;

(b) in relation to recognition or enforcement by a court in any part of the United Kingdom of—

(i) a judgment or decision given in proceedings of which a court in a State bound by a relevant instrument was seised before IP completion day;

(ii) a court settlement concluded, or authentic instrument registered, before IP completion day in a State bound by a relevant instrument,

where the question of recognition or enforcement has not arisen for consideration by the first mentioned court before IP completion day, or having so arisen, that court has not concluded its consideration before that day.

(2) The relevant instruments referred to in paragraph (1) are—

(a) the Convention on Jurisdiction and the Enforcement of Judgments in Civil and Commercial matters, signed at Brussels on 27 September 1968;

(b) the Convention on Jurisdiction and the Recognition and Enforcement of Judgments in Civil and Commercial matters, between the member States of the European Communities and the Republic of Iceland, the Kingdom of Norway and the Swiss Confederation, signed by the member States on 16 September 1988;

(c) … [Reg. 92(2)(c) omitted]

(d) the 2007 Lugano Convention;

(e) … [Reg. 92(2)(e) omitted]

(f) … [Reg. 92(2)(f) omitted]

(3) Notwithstanding the provision made by these Regulations, and subject to regulation 93, on and after IP completion day—

(a) the relevant instruments, as they are incorporated or saved by sections 3 and 4 of the European Union (Withdrawal) Act 2018, continue to have effect in relation to questions of jurisdiction, or recognition or enforcement, mentioned in paragraph (1) as if those instruments had not been revoked by these Regulations and the United Kingdom remained a member State;

(b) EU-derived domestic legislation relating to the relevant instruments, as it is saved by section 2 of the European Union (Withdrawal) Act

2018, continues to have effect in relation to questions of jurisdiction, or recognition or enforcement, mentioned in paragraph (1) as if the provision made by these Regulations in respect of that legislation had not been made and the United Kingdom remained a member State.

(4) In this regulation, a reference to "recognition" includes non-recognition if the context so requires.

(5) This regulation does not apply to a maintenance obligation or request to which the International Recovery of Maintenance (Hague Convention on the International Recovery of Child Support and Other Forms of Family Maintenance 2007) (EU Exit) Regulations 2018(**a**) apply.

Modifications of relevant instruments and EU-derived domestic legislation saved by regulation 92

93. —(1) In any case where regulation 92 applies, the relevant instruments and EU derived domestic legislation saved by regulation 92 apply with the following modifications.

(2) Where before IP completion day a court in any part of the United Kingdom (the UK court) was seised of proceedings to which a relevant instrument applies, and a court in a State bound by that relevant instrument is subsequently seised of proceedings involving the same cause of action and between the same parties, the UK court may after IP completion day decline jurisdiction if, and only if, it considers that it would be unjust not to do so.

(3) If before IP completion day a court in any part of the United Kingdom was seised of proceedings against a defendant domiciled in a State bound by a relevant instrument, and it has not been possible to transmit the document instituting the proceedings in accordance with Regulation (EC) No. 1393/2007 by reason of the exit of the United Kingdom from the European Union, then, if the defendant does not appear before the court, the court may apply whichever of the following provisions of that relevant instrument listed below as appears just—

(a) Article 26(2) or (4) of Regulation (EC) No 44/2001;
(b) Article 26(2) or (4) of the 2007 Lugano Convention;
(c) Article 28(2) or (4) of Regulation (EU) No 1215/2012.

(4) Where regulation 92(1)(b) applies, any obligation to provide or serve a certificate under any of the following provisions does not apply—

(a) Articles 54, 57 and 58 of Regulation (EC) No 44/2001;
(b) Articles 54, 57 and 58 of the 2007 Lugano Convention;
(c) Articles 53 and 60 of Regulation (EU) No 1215/2012.

(5) In this regulation, "Regulation (EC) No. 1393/2007" means Regulation (EC) No. 1393/2007 of the European Parliament and of the Council of 13 November 2007 on the service in the Member States of judicial and extrajudicial documents in civil or commercial matters (service of documents) and repealing Council Regulation (EC) No. 1348/2000.

(6) In this regulation, references to "defendant" include "defender".

Savings relating to jurisdiction, recognition and enforcement: application of Articles 67 and 69 of the withdrawal agreement

93A. Nothing in these Regulations affects the application of paragraphs 1(a) and 2(a) of Article 67 and paragraph 2 of Article 69 of the withdrawal agreement and legislation amended or revoked by these Regulations continues to have effect for the purposes of those paragraphs as if the amendments or revocations had not been made.

93B. Nothing in these Regulations affects the application of paragraph (c) of Article 68 of the withdrawal agreement and Council Decision of 28 May 2001 establishing a European Judicial Network in civil and commercial matters (2001/470/EC) continues to have effect for the purposes of that paragraph.

Savings for European Enforcement Orders and European Orders for Payment applied for, and European Small Claims Procedures commenced, before exit day

94. … [Reg. 94 omitted]

Interpretation of this Part

95. —(1) In this Part—

"relevant instrument" means an instrument mentioned in paragraph (2) of regulation 92;

"Regulation (EU) No 1215/2012" means Regulation (EU) No 1215/2012 of the European Parliament and of the Council of 12 December 2012 on Jurisdiction and the Recognition and Enforcement of Judgments in Civil and Commercial matters, including as applied by virtue of the Agreement between the European Community and the Kingdom of Denmark on Jurisdiction and the Recognition and Enforcement of Judgments in Civil and Commercial matters, of 19 October 2005;

"Regulation (EC) No 44/2001" means Council Regulation (EC) No 44/2001 on Jurisdiction and the Recognition and Enforcement of Judgments in Civil and Commercial matters, including as applied by virtue of the Agreement between the European Community and the Kingdom of Denmark on Jurisdiction and the Recognition and Enforcement of Judgments in Civil and Commercial matters, of 19 October 2005;

"the 2007 Lugano Convention" means the Convention on Jurisdiction and the Recognition and Enforcement of Judgments in Civil and Commercial matters, between the European Community and the Republic of Iceland, the Kingdom of Norway, the Swiss Confederation and the Kingdom of Denmark, signed on behalf of the Community on 30 October 2007.

(2) In this Part, a court shall be deemed to be seised—

(a) at the time when the document instituting the proceedings or an equivalent document is lodged with the court, provided that the applicant has not subsequently failed to take the steps the applicant was required to take to have service effected on the respondent; or

(b) if the document has to be served before being lodged with the court, at the time when it is received by the authority responsible for service (being the first authority receiving the document to be served), provided that the applicant has not subsequently failed to take the steps the applicant was required to take to have the document lodged with the court.

(3) In paragraph (2), references to "applicant" include "claimant" or "pursuer", and references to "respondent" include "defendant" or "defender".

(4) Nothing in this Part shall be interpreted as saving any obligation upon the United Kingdom under any of the relevant instruments to notify the Depository or the European Commission, as the case may be, of any matter, or update any such notification after exit day.

8 The Law Applicable to Contractual Obligations and Non-Contractual Obligations (Amendment etc.) (EU Exit) Regulations 2019

Part 1

Introductory

Citation and commencement

1. These Regulations may be cited as the Law Applicable to Contractual Obligations and Non-Contractual Obligations (Amendment etc.) (EU Exit) Regulations 2019 and come into force on exit day.

Part 2

Amendment of primary legislation

Amendment of the Prescription and Limitation (Scotland) Act 1973

2. For section 23A(5) of the Prescription and Limitation (Scotland) Act 1973 (application of the Rome I and II Regulations) substitute—

"(5) In subsection (4)—

(a) "the Rome I Regulation" means Regulation (EC) No. 593/2008 of the European Parliament and of the Council on the law applicable to contractual obligations (Rome I) as that Regulation has effect as retained direct EU legislation (including that Regulation as applied by regulation 4 of the Law Applicable to Contractual Obligations (Scotland) Regulations 2009), unless the proceedings are ones in respect of which Regulation (EC) No. 593/2008 has effect by virtue of Article 66 of the EU withdrawal agreement, in which case it means that Regulation as it has effect by virtue of that Article; and
(b) "the Rome II Regulation" means Regulation (EC) No. 864/2007 of the European Parliament and of the Council on the law applicable to non-contractual obligations (Rome II) as that Regulation has effect as retained direct EU legislation (including that Regulation as applied by regulation 4 of the Law Applicable to Non-Contractual

DOI: 10.4324/9781003673194-10

Obligations (Scotland) Regulations 2008), unless the proceedings are ones in respect of which Regulation (EC) No. 864/2007 has effect by virtue of Article 66 of the EU withdrawal agreement, in which case it means that Regulation as it has effect by virtue of that Article.".

Amendment of the Foreign Limitation Periods Act 1984

(2A). —(1) In section 8 of the Foreign Limitation Periods Act 1984 (disapplication of sections 1, 2 and 4 where the law applicable to limitation is determined by other instruments), for subsections (1A) and (2) substitute—

"(1A) In subsection (1) the "Rome I Regulation" means Regulation (EC) No. 593/2008 of the European Parliament and of the Council on the law applicable to contractual obligations as that Regulation has effect as retained direct EU legislation (including that Regulation as applied by regulation 5 of the Law Applicable to Contractual Obligations (England and Wales and Northern Ireland) Regulations 2009), unless the proceedings are ones in respect of which Regulation (EC) No. 593/2008 has effect by virtue of Article 66 of the EU withdrawal agreement, in which case it means that Regulation as it has effect by virtue of that Article.

(2) In subsection (1) the "Rome II Regulation" means Regulation (EC) No. 864/2007 of the European Parliament and of the Council on the law applicable to non-contractual obligations as that Regulation has effect as retained direct EU legislation (including that Regulation as applied by regulation 6 of the Law Applicable to Non-Contractual Obligations (England and Wales and Northern Ireland) Regulations 2008), unless the proceedings are ones in respect of which Regulation (EC) No. 864/2007 has effect by virtue of Article 66 of the EU withdrawal agreement, in which case it means that Regulation as it has effect by virtue of that Article.".

Amendment of the Contracts (Applicable Law) Act 1990

3. —(1) The Contracts (Applicable Law) Act 1990 is amended as follows.

(2) For section 1 (meaning of "the Conventions") substitute—

"1. **Meaning of "the Rome Convention"**

In this Act, a reference to the Rome Convention is a reference to the provisions contained in Schedule 1 (which is derived from the

Convention on the law applicable to contractual obligations opened for signature in Rome on 19th June 1980).".

(3) In section 2 (Conventions to have force of law)—

(a) for the heading substitute "Application of the Rome Convention";
(b) for subsection (1) substitute—

"(1) The Rome Convention applies to contracts made on or after 1st April 1991.";

(c) omit subsections (1A), (2) and (4);
(d) in subsection (3), for the words from "Notwithstanding" to "Conventions" substitute "The Rome Convention".

(4) In section 3 (interpretation of Conventions)—

(a) in the heading, for "Conventions" substitute "the Rome Convention";
(b) for subsection (1) substitute—

"(1) Any question as to the meaning or effect of any provision of the Rome Convention is to be decided in accordance with section 6 of the European Union (Withdrawal) Act 2018 (interpretation of retained EU law).";

(c) omit subsection (2);
(d) in subsection (3)(a)—

(i) for "Rome Convention" substitute "Convention on the law applicable to contractual obligations"; and
(ii) for "that Convention" substitute "the Rome Convention";

(e) omit subsection (3)(b) and the "and" before it.

(5) Omit section 4 (revision of Conventions).
(6) In section 4A (disapplication where the rules in the Rome I Regulation apply: England and Wales and Northern Ireland), for subsection (2) substitute—

"(2) In this section "the Rome I Regulation" means Regulation (EC) No. 593/2008 of the European Parliament and of the Council on the law applicable to contractual obligations as that Regulation has effect as retained direct EU legislation (including that Regulation as applied by regulation 5 of the Law Applicable to Contractual Obligations (England and Wales and Northern Ireland) Regulations 2009), unless the issues are ones in respect of which Regulation (EC) No. 593/2008 has effect by virtue of Article 66 of the EU withdrawal agreement, in which case it means that Regulation as it has effect by virtue of that Article.";

(7) In section 4B (disapplication where the rules in the Rome I Regulation apply: Scotland), for subsection (2) substitute—

"(2) In this section—

"the Rome I Regulation" means Regulation (EC) No. 593/2008 of the European Parliament and of the Council on the law applicable to contractual obligations as that Regulation has effect as retained direct EU legislation (including that Regulation as applied by regulation 4 of the Law Applicable to Contractual Obligations (Scotland) Regulations 2009), unless the issues are ones in respect of which Regulation (EC) No. 593/2008 has effect by virtue of Article 66 of the EU withdrawal agreement, in which case it means that Regulation as it has effect by virtue of that Article.".

(8) Omit section 8(2) and (3) (power to extend or modify the Act in relation to territories).

(9) In Schedule 1 (the Rome Convention)—

(a) in the words before Article 1 (statement as to the establishment of the Convention), omit the words from "The High Contracting Parties" to "Have agreed as follows:";

(b) in Article 1(3) (Convention to not apply to contracts of insurance covering risks in Member States)—

(i) for "Member States" substitute "United Kingdom or any Member State";

(ii) omit the words from "In order" to the end;

(c) in Article 2 (application of law of non-contracting states)—

(i) for the heading substitute "Application of law of a country outside of the United Kingdom";

(ii) for "a Contracting State" substitute "the United Kingdom or a part of the United Kingdom";

(d) omit Article 7(1) (application of mandatory rules of the law of another country);

(e) omit Article 10(1)(e) (applicable law shall govern the consequences of nullity of the contract);

(f) omit Article 17 (no retrospective effect);

(g) omit Article 19(2) (states with more than one legal system not bound to apply convention to internal disputes);

(h) in Article 20 (precedence of Community law)—

(i) in the heading, for “Community” substitute “retained EU”;

(ii) for the words from “or will be contained” to the end substitute “contained in retained EU law”;

(i) in Article 21 (relationship with other conventions), for “a Contracting State” substitute “the United Kingdom”;

(j) omit from Article 22 to the end.

(10) Omit Schedules 2 to 3B (the Luxembourg Convention, the Brussels Protocol, the Funchal Convention and the Accession Convention).

Amendment of the Private International Law (Miscellaneous Provisions) Act 1995

4. —(1) The Private International (Miscellaneous Provisions) Act 1995 is amended as follows.

(2) In section 15A (disapplication of Part III where the rules in the Rome II Regulation apply), for subsection (2) substitute—

“(2) In this section “the Rome II Regulation” means Regulation (EC) No. 864/2007 of the European Parliament and of the Council on the law applicable to non-contractual obligations as that Regulation has effect as retained direct EU legislation (including that Regulation as applied by regulation 6 of the Law Applicable to Non-Contractual Obligations (England and Wales and Northern Ireland) Regulations 2008), unless the issues are ones in respect of which Regulation (EC) No. 864/2007 has effect by virtue of Article 66 of the EU withdrawal agreement, in which case it means that Regulation as it has effect by virtue of that Article.”.

(3) In section 15B (disapplication of Part III where the rules in the Rome II Regulation apply: Scotland), for subsection (2) substitute—

“(2) In this section “the Rome II Regulation” means Regulation (EC) No. 864/2007 of the European Parliament and of the Council on the law applicable to non-contractual obligations as that Regulation has effect as retained direct EU legislation (including that Regulation as applied by regulation 4 of the Law Applicable to Non-Contractual Obligations (Scotland) Regulations 2008), unless the issues are ones in respect of which Regulation (EC) No. 864/2007 has effect by virtue of

Article 66 of the EU withdrawal agreement, in which case it means that Regulation as it has effect by virtue of that Article.".

Amendment of the Consumer Rights Act 2015

4A. — (1) The Consumer Rights Act 2015 is amended as follows.

(2) In section 32 (contracts applying law of non-EEA State) at the end of subsection (3) insert "as that Regulation has effect as retained direct EU legislation (including that Regulation as applied by regulation 5 of the Law Applicable to Contractual Obligations (England and Wales and Northern Ireland) Regulations 2009 and regulation 4 of the Law Applicable to Contractual Obligations (Scotland) Regulations 2009), unless the case is one in respect of which Regulation (EC) No. 593/2008 has effect by virtue of Article 66 of the EU withdrawal agreement, in which case see that Regulation as it has effect by virtue of that Article.".

(3) In section 74 (contracts applying law of non-EEA State) at the end of subsection (2) insert "as that Regulation has effect as retained direct EU legislation (including that Regulation as applied by regulation 5 of the Law Applicable to Contractual Obligations (England and Wales and Northern Ireland) Regulations 2009 and regulation 4 of the Law Applicable to Contractual Obligations (Scotland) Regulations 2009), unless the case is one in respect of which Regulation (EC) No. 593/2008 has effect by virtue of Article 66 of the EU withdrawal agreement, in which case see that Regulation as it has effect by virtue of that Article.

Amendment of the Foreign Limitation Periods (Northern Ireland) Order 1985

4B. [Omitted]

Part 3

Amendment of secondary legislation

5–9. [Omitted]

Part 4

Amendment of retained EU law

Amendment of the Rome I Regulation

10. — (1) Regulation (EC) No. 593/2008 of the European Parliament and of the Council of 17 June 2008 on the law applicable to contractual obligations (Rome I) is amended as follows.

(2) In Article 1 (material scope)—

(a) in paragraph 2(j), for the words beginning with "Article 2" and ending with "assurance" substitute "Article 2(1) of Directive 2009/138/EU which carry on life assurance under Article 2(3) of that Directive";

(b) for paragraph 4, substitute—

"**4.** In this Regulation, "relevant state" means the United Kingdom and—

(a) in Article 3(4) and Article 7, all the Member States;

(b) in all other Articles, the Member States to which Regulation (EC) No. 593/2008 of the European Parliament and of the Council of 17 June 2008 on the law applicable to contractual obligations (Rome I), as it has effect in EU law and as amended from time to time, applies.".

(3) In Article 2 (universal application), for "a Member State", substitute "the United Kingdom or a part of the United Kingdom".

(4) In Article 3(4) (parties' choice of applicable law shall not prejudice application of community law under certain circumstances)—

(a) for "Member States" substitute "relevant states";

(b) for "Member State", in the first place it appears, substitute "relevant state";

(c) for "Community law, where appropriate as implemented in the Member State of the forum,", substitute "retained EU law".

(5) In Article 4(1)(h) (applicable law in the absence of choice), for "by Article 4(1), point (17) of Directive 2004/39/EC" substitute "in Part 1 of Schedule 2 to the Financial Services and Markets Act 2000 (Regulated Activities) Order 2001".

(6) In Article 6(4) (consumer contracts: general rules not to apply in certain circumstances)—

(a) in point (b), for the words from "Council" to the end substitute "Directive (EU) 2015/2302 of the European Parliament and of the Council of 25 November 2015 on package travel and linked travel arrangements";

(b) in point (c), for "Directive 94/47/EC" substitute "Directive 2008/122/EC".

(7) In Article 7 (insurance contracts)—

(a) in paragraph 1—

(i) for "Member State" substitute "relevant state";
(ii) for "Member States" substitute "relevant states";

(b) in paragraph 2, for the words from "Article 5(d)" to "life assurance" substitute "Article 13(27) of Directive 2009/138/EU";
(c) in paragraph 3—

(i) for "Member State" in each place it appears substitute "relevant state";
(ii) for "Member States" in each place it appears substitute "relevant states";

(d) in paragraph 4—

(i) in the words before point (a) for "rules" substitute "rule";
(ii) for "Member State" in each place it appears substitute "relevant state";
(iii) omit point (b);

(e) in paragraph 5, for "Member State" in both places it appears substitute "relevant state";
(f) in paragraph 6—

(i) for the words from "Article 2(d)" to "services" substitute "Article 13(13) of Directive 2009/138/EU";
(ii) for "Article 1(1)(g) of Directive 2002/83/EC" substitute "Article 13(14) of Directive 2009/138/EU".

(8) Omit Article 22(2) (Member States comprising territorial units with different rules of law not required to apply the Regulation).
(9) In Article 23 (relationship with other provisions of Community law), and in the heading to that Article, for "Community law", substitute "retained EU law".
(10) In Article 24 (relationship with Rome Convention)—

(a) for paragraph 1 substitute—

"**1.** This Regulation replaces the provision made by section 2 of, and Schedule 1 to, the Contracts (Applicable Law) Act 1990.".

(b) in paragraph 2 for "provisions of the Rome Convention" substitute "provision made by section 2 of, and Schedule 1 to, the Contracts (Applicable Law) Act 1990" and for "that" substitute "the Rome".

(11) In Article 25 (relationship with existing international conventions)—

(a) in paragraph 1—

(i) for "one or more Member States are parties", substitute "the United Kingdom was a party";
(ii) for "is adopted" substitute "was adopted";

(b) in paragraph 2, for "Member States" substitute "relevant states".

(12) Omit Articles 26 and 27 (list of conventions and review clause).
(12A) For Article 28 (application in time) substitute—

"*Article 28*

Application in time

1. Subject to paragraph 2, this Regulation shall apply to contracts concluded on or after IP completion day.
2. In the case of conflicts between the laws of—

(a) different parts of the United Kingdom, or
(b) one or more parts of the United Kingdom and Gibraltar,

this Regulation shall apply to contracts concluded on or after 17 December 2009.".

(13) Omit from Article 29 (entry into force and application) to the end.

Amendment of the Rome II Regulation

11. (1) Regulation (EC) No 864/2007 of the European Parliament and of the Council of 11 July 2007 on the law applicable to non-contractual obligations (Rome II) is amended as follows.

(2) In Article 1(4) (scope), for "'Member State' shall mean", substitute ""“relevant state" means the United Kingdom or".
(3) In Article 3 (universal application), for "a Member State", substitute "the United Kingdom or a part of the United Kingdom".
(4) In Article 6(3)(b) (unfair competition and acts restricting free competition: claimant may choose court seised under certain circumstances)—

(a) for "the court of the domicile of the defendant" substitute "a court in a part of the United Kingdom";
(b) for "that Member State", substitute "the United Kingdom";
(c) for "Member State of that court", substitute "United Kingdom".

(5) In Article 8 (infringement of intellectual property rights), omit paragraph 2.]
(6) In Article 14(3) (parties' choice of applicable law shall not prejudice application of Community law under certain circumstances)—

(a) for "the Member States" substitute "relevant states";
(b) for "Member State", in the first place it appears, substitute "relevant state";
(c) for "provisions of Community law, where appropriate as implemented in the Member State of the forum,", substitute "retained EU law".

(7) Omit Article 25(2) (Member States containing territorial units with different rules of law not required to apply the Regulation).
(8) In Article 27 (relationship with other provisions of Community law), and in the heading to that Article, for "Community law", substitute "retained EU law".
(9) In Article 28 (relationship with existing international conventions)—

(a) in paragraph 1—

(i) for "one or more Member States are parties", substitute "the United Kingdom was a party";
(ii) for "is adopted" substitute "was adopted";

(b) in paragraph 2, for "Member States" substitute "relevant states".

(10) Omit Articles 29 and 30 (list of conventions and review clause).
(11) For Article 31 (application in time) substitute—

"*Article 31*

Application in time

1. Subject to paragraph 2, this Regulation shall apply to events giving rise to damage which occur on or after IP completion day.
2. In the case of conflicts between the laws of—

(a) different parts of the United Kingdom, or
(b) one or more parts of the United Kingdom and Gibraltar,

this Regulation shall apply to events giving rise to damage which occur on or after 11 January 2009.".

(12) Omit from Article 32 (date of application) to the end.

Revocation of Regulation EC No 662/2009

12. Regulation EC No 662/2009 of the European Parliament and of the Council of 13 July 2009 establishing a procedure for the negotiation and conclusion of agreements between Member States and third countries on particular matters concerning the law applicable to contractual and non-contractual obligations is revoked.

Section III

Conventions

9 Convention on Choice of Court Agreements, 2005

C – scope and definitions

Article 1

Scope

(1) This Convention shall apply in international cases to exclusive choice of court agreements concluded in civil or commercial matters.

(2) For the purposes of Chapter II, a case is international unless the parties are resident in the same Contracting State and the relationship of the parties and all other elements relevant to the dispute, regardless of the location of the chosen court, are connected only with that State.

(3) For the purposes of Chapter III, a case is international where recognition or enforcement of a foreign judgment is sought.

Article 2

Exclusions from scope

(1) This Convention shall not apply to exclusive choice of court agreements –

- a) to which a natural person acting primarily for personal, family or household purposes (a consumer) is a party;
- b) relating to contracts of employment, including collective agreements.

(2) This Convention shall not apply to the following matters –

- a) the status and legal capacity of natural persons;
- b) maintenance obligations;
- c) other family law matters, including matrimonial property regimes and other rights or obligations arising out of marriage or similar relationships;
- d) wills and succession;
- e) insolvency, composition and analogous matters;

DOI: 10.4324/9781003673194-12

f) the carriage of passengers and goods;
g) marine pollution, limitation of liability for maritime claims, general average, and emergency towage and salvage;
h) anti-trust (competition) matters;
i) liability for nuclear damage;
j) claims for personal injury brought by or on behalf of natural persons;
k) tort or delict claims for damage to tangible property that do not arise from a contractual relationship;
l) rights *in rem* in immovable property, and tenancies of immovable property;
m) the validity, nullity, or dissolution of legal persons, and the validity of decisions of their organs;
n) the validity of intellectual property rights other than copyright and related rights;
o) infringement of intellectual property rights other than copyright and related rights, except where infringement proceedings are brought for breach of a contract between the parties relating to such rights, or could have been brought for breach of that contract;
p) the validity of entries in public registers.

(3) Notwithstanding paragraph 2, proceedings are not excluded from the scope of this Convention where a matter excluded under that paragraph arises merely as a preliminary question and not as an object of the proceedings. In particular, the mere fact that a matter excluded under paragraph 2 arises by way of defence does not exclude proceedings from the Convention, if that matter is not an object of the proceedings.
(4) This Convention shall not apply to arbitration and related proceedings.
(5) Proceedings are not excluded from the scope of this Convention by the mere fact that a State, including a government, a governmental agency or any person acting for a State, is a party thereto.
(6) Nothing in this Convention shall affect privileges and immunities of States or of international organisations, in respect of themselves and of their property.

Article 3

Exclusive choice of court agreements

For the purposes of this Convention –

a) “exclusive choice of court agreement” means an agreement concluded by two or more parties that meets the requirements of paragraph *c)* and designates, for the purpose of deciding disputes which have arisen or may arise in connection with a particular legal relationship, the courts of one Contracting State or one or more specific courts of one Contracting State to the exclusion of the jurisdiction of any other courts;

b) a choice of court agreement which designates the courts of one Contracting State or one or more specific courts of one Contracting State shall be deemed to be exclusive unless the parties have expressly provided otherwise;

c) an exclusive choice of court agreement must be concluded or documented –

   i) in writing; or
   ii) by any other means of communication which renders information accessible so as to be usable for subsequent reference;

d) an exclusive choice of court agreement that forms part of a contract shall be treated as an agreement independent of the other terms of the contract. The validity of the exclusive choice of court agreement cannot be contested solely on the ground that the contract is not valid.

Article 4

Other definitions

(1) In this Convention, "judgment" means any decision on the merits given by a court, whatever it may be called, including a decree or order, and a determination of costs or expenses by the court (including an officer of the court), provided that the determination relates to a decision on the merits which may be recognised or enforced under this Convention. An interim measure of protection is not a judgment.

(2) For the purposes of this Convention, an entity or person other than a natural person shall be considered to be resident in the State –

   a) where it has its statutory seat;
   b) under whose law it was incorporated or formed;
   c) where it has its central administration; or
   d) where it has its principal place of business.

Chapter II – jurisdiction

Article 5

Jurisdiction of the chosen court

(1) The court or courts of a Contracting State designated in an exclusive choice of court agreement shall have jurisdiction to decide a dispute to which the agreement applies, unless the agreement is null and void under the law of that State.

(2) A court that has jurisdiction under paragraph 1 shall not decline to exercise jurisdiction on the ground that the dispute should be decided in a court of another State.

(3) The preceding paragraphs shall not affect rules –

a) on jurisdiction related to subject matter or to the value of the claim;
b) on the internal allocation of jurisdiction among the courts of a Contracting State. However, where the chosen court has discretion as to whether to transfer a case, due consideration should be given to the choice of the parties.

Article 6

Obligations of a court not chosen

A court of a Contracting State other than that of the chosen court shall suspend or dismiss proceedings to which an exclusive choice of court agreement applies unless –

a) the agreement is null and void under the law of the State of the chosen court;
b) a party lacked the capacity to conclude the agreement under the law of the State of the court seised;
c) giving effect to the agreement would lead to a manifest injustice or would be manifestly contrary to the public policy of the State of the court seised;
d) for exceptional reasons beyond the control of the parties, the agreement cannot reasonably be performed; or
e) the chosen court has decided not to hear the case.

Article 7

Interim measures of protection

Interim measures of protection are not governed by this Convention. This Convention neither requires nor precludes the grant, refusal or termination of interim measures of protection by a court of a Contracting State and does not affect whether or not a party may request or a court should grant, refuse or terminate such measures.

Chapter III – recognition and enforcement

Article 8

Recognition and enforcement

(1) A judgment given by a court of a Contracting State designated in an exclusive choice of court agreement shall be recognised and enforced in

other Contracting States in accordance with this Chapter. Recognition or enforcement may be refused only on the grounds specified in this Convention.

(2) Without prejudice to such review as is necessary for the application of the provisions of this Chapter, there shall be no review of the merits of the judgment given by the court of origin. The court addressed shall be bound by the findings of fact on which the court of origin based its jurisdiction, unless the judgment was given by default.

(3) A judgment shall be recognised only if it has effect in the State of origin, and shall be enforced only if it is enforceable in the State of origin.

(4) Recognition or enforcement may be postponed or refused if the judgment is the subject of review in the State of origin or if the time limit for seeking ordinary review has not expired. A refusal does not prevent a subsequent application for recognition or enforcement of the judgment.

(5) This Article shall also apply to a judgment given by a court of a Contracting State pursuant to a transfer of the case from the chosen court in that Contracting State as permitted by Article 5, paragraph 3. However, where the chosen court had discretion as to whether to transfer the case to another court, recognition or enforcement of the judgment may be refused against a party who objected to the transfer in a timely manner in the State of origin.

Article 9

Refusal of recognition or enforcement

Recognition or enforcement may be refused if –

a) the agreement was null and void under the law of the State of the chosen court, unless the chosen court has determined that the agreement is valid;
b) a party lacked the capacity to conclude the agreement under the law of the requested State;
c) the document which instituted the proceedings or an equivalent document, including the essential elements of the claim,

    i) was not notified to the defendant in sufficient time and in such a way as to enable him to arrange for his defence, unless the defendant entered an appearance and presented his case without contesting notification in the court of origin, provided that the law of the State of origin permitted notification to be contested; or
    ii) was notified to the defendant in the requested State in a manner that is incompatible with fundamental principles of the requested State concerning service of documents;

d) the judgment was obtained by fraud in connection with a matter of procedure;

e) recognition or enforcement would be manifestly incompatible with the public policy of the requested State, including situations where the specific proceedings leading to the judgment were incompatible with fundamental principles of procedural fairness of that State;

f) the judgment is inconsistent with a judgment given in the requested State in a dispute between the same parties; or

g) the judgment is inconsistent with an earlier judgment given in another State between the same parties on the same cause of action, provided that the earlier judgment fulfils the conditions necessary for its recognition in the requested State.

Article 10

Preliminary questions

(1) Where a matter excluded under Article 2, paragraph 2, or under Article 21, arose as a preliminary question, the ruling on that question shall not be recognised or enforced under this Convention.

(2) Recognition or enforcement of a judgment may be refused if, and to the extent that, the judgment was based on a ruling on a matter excluded under Article 2, paragraph 2.

(3) However, in the case of a ruling on the validity of an intellectual property right other than copyright or a related right, recognition or enforcement of a judgment may be refused or postponed under the preceding paragraph only where –

   a) that ruling is inconsistent with a judgment or a decision of a competent authority on that matter given in the State under the law of which the intellectual property right arose; or

   b) proceedings concerning the validity of the intellectual property right are pending in that State.

(4) Recognition or enforcement of a judgment may be refused if, and to the extent that, the judgment was based on a ruling on a matter excluded pursuant to a declaration made by the requested State under Article 21.

Article 11

Damages

(1) Recognition or enforcement of a judgment may be refused if, and to the extent that, the judgment awards damages, including exemplary or punitive damages, that do not compensate a party for actual loss or harm suffered.

(2) The court addressed shall take into account whether and to what extent the damages awarded by the court of origin serve to cover costs and expenses relating to the proceedings.

Article 12

*Judicial settlements (*transactions judiciaires*)*

Judicial settlements (*transactions judiciaires*) which a court of a Contracting State designated in an exclusive choice of court agreement has approved, or which have been concluded before that court in the course of proceedings, and which are enforceable in the same manner as a judgment in the State of origin, shall be enforced under this Convention in the same manner as a judgment.

Article 13

Documents to be produced

(1) The party seeking recognition or applying for enforcement shall produce –

a) a complete and certified copy of the judgment;
b) the exclusive choice of court agreement, a certified copy thereof, or other evidence of its existence;
c) if the judgment was given by default, the original or a certified copy of a document establishing that the document which instituted the proceedings or an equivalent document was notified to the defaulting party;
d) any documents necessary to establish that the judgment has effect or, where applicable, is enforceable in the State of origin;
e) in the case referred to in Article 12, a certificate of a court of the State of origin that the judicial settlement or a part of it is enforceable in the same manner as a judgment in the State of origin.

(2) If the terms of the judgment do not permit the court addressed to verify whether the conditions of this Chapter have been complied with, that court may require any necessary documents.
(3) An application for recognition or enforcement may be accompanied by a document, issued by a court (including an officer of the court) of the State of origin, in the form recommended and published by the Hague Conference on Private International Law.
(4) If the documents referred to in this Article are not in an official language of the requested State, they shall be accompanied by a certified translation into an official language, unless the law of the requested State provides otherwise.

Article 14

Procedure

The procedure for recognition, declaration of enforceability or registration for enforcement, and the enforcement of the judgment, are governed by the law of the requested State unless this Convention provides otherwise. The court addressed shall act expeditiously.

Article 15

Severability

Recognition or enforcement of a severable part of a judgment shall be granted where recognition or enforcement of that part is applied for, or only part of the judgment is capable of being recognised or enforced under this Convention.

Chapter IV – general clauses

Article 16

Transitional provisions

(1) This Convention shall apply to exclusive choice of court agreements concluded after its entry into force for the State of the chosen court.
(2) This Convention shall not apply to proceedings instituted before its entry into force for the State of the court seised.

Article 17

Contracts of insurance and reinsurance

(1) Proceedings under a contract of insurance or reinsurance are not excluded from the scope of this Convention on the ground that the contract of insurance or reinsurance relates to a matter to which this Convention does not apply.
(2) Recognition and enforcement of a judgment in respect of liability under the terms of a contract of insurance or reinsurance may not be limited or refused on the ground that the liability under that contract includes liability to indemnify the insured or reinsured in respect of –

    a) a matter to which this Convention does not apply; or
    b) an award of damages to which Article 11 might apply.

Article 18

No legalisation

All documents forwarded or delivered under this Convention shall be exempt from legalisation or any analogous formality, including an Apostille.

Article 19

Declarations limiting jurisdiction

A State may declare that its courts may refuse to determine disputes to which an exclusive choice of court agreement applies if, except for the location of the chosen court, there is no connection between that State and the parties or the dispute.

Article 20

Declarations limiting recognition and enforcement

A State may declare that its courts may refuse to recognise or enforce a judgment given by a court of another Contracting State if the parties were resident in the requested State, and the relationship of the parties and all other elements relevant to the dispute, other than the location of the chosen court, were connected only with the requested State.

Article 21

Declarations with respect to specific matters

(1) Where a State has a strong interest in not applying this Convention to a specific matter, that State may declare that it will not apply the Convention to that matter. The State making such a declaration shall ensure that the declaration is no broader than necessary and that the specific matter excluded is clearly and precisely defined.

(2) With regard to that matter, the Convention shall not apply –

  a) in the Contracting State that made the declaration;
  b) in other Contracting States, where an exclusive choice of court agreement designates the courts, or one or more specific courts, of the State that made the declaration.

Article 22

Reciprocal declarations on non-exclusive choice of court agreements

(1) A Contracting State may declare that its courts will recognise and enforce judgments given by courts of other Contracting States designated in a choice of court agreement concluded by two or more parties that meets the requirements of Article 3, paragraph *c)*, and designates, for the purpose of deciding disputes which have arisen or may arise in connection with a particular legal relationship, a court or courts of one or more Contracting States (a non-exclusive choice of court agreement).

(2) Where recognition or enforcement of a judgment given in a Contracting State that has made such a declaration is sought in another Contracting State that has made such a declaration, the judgment shall be recognised and enforced under this Convention, if –

a) the court of origin was designated in a non-exclusive choice of court agreement;
b) there exists neither a judgment given by any other court before which proceedings could be brought in accordance with the non-exclusive choice of court agreement, nor a proceeding pending between the same parties in any other such court on the same cause of action; and
c) the court of origin was the court first seised.

Article 23

Uniform interpretation

In the interpretation of this Convention, regard shall be had to its international character and to the need to promote uniformity in its application.

Article 24

Review of operation of the Convention

The Secretary General of the Hague Conference on Private International Law shall at regular intervals make arrangements for –

a) review of the operation of this Convention, including any declarations; and
b) consideration of whether any amendments to this Convention are desirable.

Article 25

Non-unified legal systems

(1) In relation to a Contracting State in which two or more systems of law apply in different territorial units with regard to any matter dealt with in this Convention –

a) any reference to the law or procedure of a State shall be construed as referring, where appropriate, to the law or procedure in force in the relevant territorial unit;
b) any reference to residence in a State shall be construed as referring, where appropriate, to residence in the relevant territorial unit;

c) any reference to the court or courts of a State shall be construed as referring, where appropriate, to the court or courts in the relevant territorial unit;
d) any reference to a connection with a State shall be construed as referring, where appropriate, to a connection with the relevant territorial unit.

(2) Notwithstanding the preceding paragraph, a Contracting State with two or more territorial units in which different systems of law apply shall not be bound to apply this Convention to situations which involve solely such different territorial units.
(3) A court in a territorial unit of a Contracting State with two or more territorial units in which different systems of law apply shall not be bound to recognise or enforce a judgment from another Contracting State solely because the judgment has been recognised or enforced in another territorial unit of the same Contracting State under this Convention.
(4) This Article shall not apply to a Regional Economic Integration Organisation.

Article 26

Relationship with other international instruments

(1) This Convention shall be interpreted so far as possible to be compatible with other treaties in force for Contracting States, whether concluded before or after this Convention.
(2) This Convention shall not affect the application by a Contracting State of a treaty, whether concluded before or after this Convention, in cases where none of the parties is resident in a Contracting State that is not a Party to the treaty.
(3) This Convention shall not affect the application by a Contracting State of a treaty that was concluded before this Convention entered into force for that Contracting State, if applying this Convention would be inconsistent with the obligations of that Contracting State to any non Contracting State. This paragraph shall also apply to treaties that revise or replace a treaty concluded before this Convention entered into force for that Contracting State, except to the extent that the revision or replacement creates new inconsistencies with this Convention.
(4) This Convention shall not affect the application by a Contracting State of a treaty, whether concluded before or after this Convention, for the purposes of obtaining recognition or enforcement of a judgment given by a court of a Contracting State that is also a Party to that treaty. However, the judgment shall not be recognised or enforced to a lesser extent than under this Convention.

(5) This Convention shall not affect the application by a Contracting State of a treaty which, in relation to a specific matter, governs jurisdiction or the recognition or enforcement of judgments, even if concluded after this Convention and even if all States concerned are Parties to this Convention. This paragraph shall apply only if the Contracting State has made a declaration in respect of the treaty under this paragraph. In the case of such a declaration, other Contracting States shall not be obliged to apply this Convention to that specific matter to the extent of any inconsistency, where an exclusive choice of court agreement designates the courts, or one or more specific courts, of the Contracting State that made the declaration.

(6) This Convention shall not affect the application of the rules of a Regional Economic Integration Organisation that is a Party to this Convention, whether adopted before or after this Convention –

a) where none of the parties is resident in a Contracting State that is not a Member State of the Regional Economic Integration Organisation;

b) as concerns the recognition or enforcement of judgments as between Member States of the Regional Economic Integration Organisation.

Chapter V – final clauses

Articles 27–34 [Omitted]

10 Convention on the Recognition and Enforcement of Foreign Judgments in Civil or Commercial Matters, 2019

Chapter I – scope and definitions

Article 1

Scope

1. This Convention shall apply to the recognition and enforcement of judgments in civil or commercial matters. It shall not extend in particular to revenue, customs or administrative matters.
2. This Convention shall apply to the recognition and enforcement in one Contracting State of a judgment given by a court of another Contracting State.

Article 2

Exclusions from scope

1. This Convention shall not apply to the following matters –

   (a) the status and legal capacity of natural persons;
   (b) maintenance obligations;
   (c) other family law matters, including matrimonial property regimes and other rights or obligations arising out of marriage or similar relationships;
   (d) wills and succession;
   (e) insolvency, composition, resolution of financial institutions, and analogous matters;
   (f) the carriage of passengers and goods;
   (g) transboundary marine pollution, marine pollution in areas beyond national jurisdiction, ship-source marine pollution, limitation of liability for maritime claims, and general average;
   (h) liability for nuclear damage;

DOI: 10.4324/9781003673194-13

(i) the validity, nullity, or dissolution of legal persons or associations of natural or legal persons, and the validity of decisions of their organs;
(j) the validity of entries in public registers;
(k) defamation;
(l) privacy;
(m) intellectual property;
(n) activities of armed forces, including the activities of their personnel in the exercise of their official duties;
(o) law enforcement activities, including the activities of law enforcement personnel in the exercise of their official duties;
(p) anti-trust (competition) matters, except where the judgment is based on conduct that constitutes an anti-competitive agreement or concerted practice among actual or potential competitors to fix prices, make rigged bids, establish output restrictions or quotas, or divide markets by allocating customers, suppliers, territories or lines of commerce, and where such conduct and its effect both occurred in the State of origin;
(q) sovereign debt restructuring through unilateral State measures.

2. A judgment is not excluded from the scope of this Convention where a matter to which this Convention does not apply arose merely as a preliminary question in the proceedings in which the judgment was given, and not as an object of the proceedings. In particular, the mere fact that such a matter arose by way of defence does not exclude a judgment from the Convention, if that matter was not an object of the proceedings.
3. This Convention shall not apply to arbitration and related proceedings.
4. A judgment is not excluded from the scope of this Convention by the mere fact that a State, including a government, a governmental agency or any person acting for a State, was a party to the proceedings.
5. Nothing in this Convention shall affect privileges and immunities of States or of international organisations, in respect of themselves and of their property.

Article 3

Definitions

1. In this Convention –

(a) "defendant" means a person against whom the claim or counterclaim was brought in the State of origin;
(b) "judgment" means any decision on the merits given by a court, whatever that decision may be called, including a decree or order, and a determination of costs or expenses of the proceedings by the

court (including an officer of the court), provided that the determination relates to a decision on the merits which may be recognised or enforced under this Convention. An interim measure of protection is not a judgment.

2. An entity or person other than a natural person shall be considered to be habitually resident in the State –

   (a) where it has its statutory seat;
   (b) under the law of which it was incorporated or formed;
   (c) where it has its central administration; or
   (d) where it has its principal place of business.

Chapter II – recognition and enforcement

Article 4

General provisions

1. A judgment given by a court of a Contracting State (State of origin) shall be recognised and enforced in another Contracting State (requested State) in accordance with the provisions of this Chapter. Recognition or enforcement may be refused only on the grounds specified in this Convention.
2. There shall be no review of the merits of the judgment in the requested State. There may only be such consideration as is necessary for the application of this Convention.
3. A judgment shall be recognised only if it has effect in the State of origin, and shall be enforced only if it is enforceable in the State of origin.
4. Recognition or enforcement may be postponed or refused if the judgment referred to under paragraph 3 is the subject of review in the State of origin or if the time limit for seeking ordinary review has not expired. A refusal does not prevent a subsequent application for recognition or enforcement of the judgment.

Article 5

Bases for recognition and enforcement

1. A judgment is eligible for recognition and enforcement if one of the following requirements is met –

   (a) the person against whom recognition or enforcement is sought was habitually resident in the State of origin at the time that person became a party to the proceedings in the court of origin;

(b) the natural person against whom recognition or enforcement is sought had their principal place of business in the State of origin at the time that person became a party to the proceedings in the court of origin and the claim on which the judgment is based arose out of the activities of that business;
(c) the person against whom recognition or enforcement is sought is the person that brought the claim, other than a counterclaim, on which the judgment is based;
(d) the defendant maintained a branch, agency, or other establishment without separate legal personality in the State of origin at the time that person became a party to the proceedings in the court of origin, and the claim on which the judgment is based arose out of the activities of that branch, agency, or establishment;
(e) the defendant expressly consented to the jurisdiction of the court of origin in the course of the proceedings in which the judgment was given;
(f) the defendant argued on the merits before the court of origin without contesting jurisdiction within the timeframe provided in the law of the State of origin, unless it is evident that an objection to jurisdiction or to the exercise of jurisdiction would not have succeeded under that law;
(g) the judgment ruled on a contractual obligation and it was given by a court of the State in which performance of that obligation took place, or should have taken place, in accordance with

   (i) the agreement of the parties, or
   (ii) the law applicable to the contract, in the absence of an agreed place of performance, unless the activities of the defendant in relation to the transaction clearly did not constitute a purposeful and substantial connection to that State;

(h) the judgment ruled on a lease of immovable property (tenancy) and it was given by a court of the State in which the property is situated;
(i) the judgment ruled against the defendant on a contractual obligation secured by a right *in rem* in immovable property located in the State of origin, if the contractual claim was brought together with a claim against the same defendant relating to that right *in rem*;
(j) the judgment ruled on a non-contractual obligation arising from death, physical injury, damage to or loss of tangible property, and the act or omission directly causing such harm occurred in the State of origin, irrespective of where that harm occurred;
(k) the judgment concerns the validity, construction, effects, administration or variation of a trust created voluntarily and evidenced in writing, and –

(i) at the time the proceedings were instituted, the State of origin was designated in the trust instrument as a State in the courts of which disputes about such matters are to be determined; or
(ii) at the time the proceedings were instituted, the State of origin was expressly or impliedly designated in the trust instrument as the State in which the principal place of administration of the trust is situated.

This sub-paragraph only applies to judgments regarding internal aspects of a trust between persons who are or were within the trust relationship;

(l) the judgment ruled on a counterclaim –

(i) to the extent that it was in favour of the counterclaimant, provided that the counterclaim arose out of the same transaction or occurrence as the claim; or
(ii) to the extent that it was against the counterclaimant, unless the law of the State of origin required the counterclaim to be filed in order to avoid preclusion;

(m) the judgment was given by a court designated in an agreement concluded or documented in writing or by any other means of communication which renders information accessible so as to be usable for subsequent reference, other than an exclusive choice of court agreement.

For the purposes of this sub-paragraph, an "exclusive choice of court agreement" means an agreement concluded by two or more parties that designates, for the purpose of deciding disputes which have arisen or may arise in connection with a particular legal relationship, the courts of one State or one or more specific courts of one State to the exclusion of the jurisdiction of any other courts.

2. If recognition or enforcement is sought against a natural person acting primarily for personal, family or household purposes (a consumer) in matters relating to a consumer contract, or against an employee in matters relating to the employee's contract of employment –

(a) paragraph 1(e) applies only if the consent was addressed to the court, orally or in writing;
(b) paragraph 1(f), (g) and (m) do not apply.

3. Paragraph 1 does not apply to a judgment that ruled on a residential lease of immovable property (tenancy) or ruled on the registration of immovable property. Such a judgment is eligible for recognition and enforcement only if it was given by a court of the State where the property is situated.

Article 6

Exclusive basis for recognition and enforcement

Notwithstanding Article 5, a judgment that ruled on rights *in rem* in immovable property shall be recognised and enforced if and only if the property is situated in the State of origin.

Article 7

Refusal of recognition and enforcement

1. Recognition or enforcement may be refused if –

    (a) the document which instituted the proceedings or an equivalent document, including a statement of the essential elements of the claim –

        (i) was not notified to the defendant in sufficient time and in such a way as to enable them to arrange for their defence, unless the defendant entered an appearance and presented their case without contesting notification in the court of origin, provided that the law of the State of origin permitted notification to be contested; or

        (ii) was notified to the defendant in the requested State in a manner that is incompatible with fundamental principles of the requested State concerning service of documents; (b) the judgment was obtained by fraud;

    (c) recognition or enforcement would be manifestly incompatible with the public policy of the requested State, including situations where the specific proceedings leading to the judgment were incompatible with fundamental principles of procedural fairness of that State and situations involving infringements of security or sovereignty of that State;

    (d) the proceedings in the court of origin were contrary to an agreement, or a designation in a trust instrument, under which the dispute in question was to be determined in a court of a State other than the State of origin;

    (e) the judgment is inconsistent with a judgment given by a court of the requested State in a dispute between the same parties; or

    (f) the judgment is inconsistent with an earlier judgment given by a court of another State between the same parties on the same subject matter, provided that the earlier judgment fulfils the conditions necessary for its recognition in the requested State.

2. Recognition or enforcement may be postponed or refused if proceedings between the same parties on the same subject matter are pending before a court of the requested State, where –
   (a) the court of the requested State was seised before the court of origin; and
   (b) there is a close connection between the dispute and the requested State.

A refusal under this paragraph does not prevent a subsequent application for recognition or enforcement of the judgment.

Article 8

Preliminary questions

1. A ruling on a preliminary question shall not be recognised or enforced under this Convention if the ruling is on a matter to which this Convention does not apply or on a matter referred to in Article 6 on which a court of a State other than the State referred to in that Article ruled.
2. Recognition or enforcement of a judgment may be refused if, and to the extent that, the judgment was based on a ruling on a matter to which this Convention does not apply, or on a matter referred to in Article 6 on which a court of a State other than the State referred to in that Article ruled.

Article 9

Severability

Recognition or enforcement of a severable part of a judgment shall be granted where recognition or enforcement of that part is applied for, or only part of the judgment is capable of being recognised or enforced under this Convention.

Article 10

Damages

1. Recognition or enforcement of a judgment may be refused if, and to the extent that, the judgment awards damages, including exemplary or punitive damages, that do not compensate a party for actual loss or harm suffered.
2. The court addressed shall take into account whether and to what extent the damages awarded by the court of origin serve to cover costs and expenses relating to the proceedings.

Article 11

Judicial settlements *(transactions judiciaires)*

Judicial settlements (*transactions judiciaires*) which a court of a Contracting State has approved, or which have been concluded in the course of proceedings before a court of a Contracting State, and which are enforceable in the same manner as a judgment in the State of origin, shall be enforced under this Convention in the same manner as a judgment.

Article 12

Documents to be produced

1. The party seeking recognition or applying for enforcement shall produce –

   (a) a complete and certified copy of the judgment;
   (b) if the judgment was given by default, the original or a certified copy of a document establishing that the document which instituted the proceedings or an equivalent document was notified to the defaulting party;
   (c) any documents necessary to establish that the judgment has effect or, where applicable, is enforceable in the State of origin;
   (d) in the case referred to in Article 11, a certificate of a court (including an officer of the court) of the State of origin stating that the judicial settlement or a part of it is enforceable in the same manner as a judgment in the State of origin.

2. If the terms of the judgment do not permit the court addressed to verify whether the conditions of this Chapter have been complied with, that court may require any necessary documents.
3. An application for recognition or enforcement may be accompanied by a document relating to the judgment, issued by a court (including an officer of the court) of the State of origin, in the form recommended and published by the Hague Conference on Private International Law.
4. If the documents referred to in this Article are not in an official language of the requested State, they shall be accompanied by a certified translation into an official language, unless the law of the requested State provides otherwise.

Article 13

Procedure

1. The procedure for recognition, declaration of enforceability or registration for enforcement, and the enforcement of the judgment, are governed by the law of the requested State unless this Convention provides otherwise. The court of the requested State shall act expeditiously.

2. The court of the requested State shall not refuse the recognition or enforcement of a judgment under this Convention on the ground that recognition or enforcement should be sought in another State.

Article 14

Costs of proceedings

1. No security, bond or deposit, however described, shall be required from a party who in one Contracting State applies for enforcement of a judgment given by a court of another Contracting State on the sole ground that such party is a foreign national or is not domiciled or resident in the State in which enforcement is sought.
2. An order for payment of costs or expenses of proceedings, made in a Contracting State against any person exempt from requirements as to security, bond, or deposit by virtue of paragraph 1 or of the law of the State where proceedings have been instituted, shall, on the application of the person entitled to the benefit of the order, be rendered enforceable in any other Contracting State.
3. A State may declare that it shall not apply paragraph 1 or designate by a declaration which of its courts shall not apply paragraph 1.

Article 15

Recognition and enforcement under national law

Subject to Article 6, this Convention does not prevent the recognition or enforcement of judgments under national law.

Chapter III – general clauses

Article 16

Transitional provision

This Convention shall apply to the recognition and enforcement of judgments if, at the time the proceedings were instituted in the State of origin, the Convention had effect between that State and the requested State.

Article 17

Declarations limiting recognition and enforcement

A State may declare that its courts may refuse to recognise or enforce a judgment given by a court of another Contracting State if the parties were resident in the requested State, and the relationship of the parties and all other elements relevant to the dispute, other than the location of the court of origin, were connected only with the requested State.

Article 18

Declarations with respect to specific matters

1. Where a State has a strong interest in not applying this Convention to a specific matter, that State may declare that it will not apply the Convention to that matter. The State making such a declaration shall ensure that the declaration is no broader than necessary and that the specific matter excluded is clearly and precisely defined.
2. With regard to that matter, the Convention shall not apply –

   (a) in the Contracting State that made the declaration;
   (b) in other Contracting States, where recognition or enforcement of a judgment given by a court of a Contracting State that made the declaration is sought.

Article 19

Declarations with respect to judgments pertaining to a State

1. A State may declare that it shall not apply this Convention to judgments arising from proceedings to which any of the following is a party –

   (a) that State, or a natural person acting for that State; or
   (b) a government agency of that State, or a natural person acting for such a government agency.

The State making such a declaration shall ensure that the declaration is no broader than necessary and that the exclusion from scope is clearly and precisely defined. The declaration shall not distinguish between judgments where the State, a government agency of that State or a natural person acting for either of them is a defendant or claimant in the proceedings before the court of origin.

2. Recognition or enforcement of a judgment given by a court of a State that made a declaration pursuant to paragraph 1 may be refused if the judgment arose from proceedings to which either the State that made the declaration or the requested State, one of their government agencies or a natural person acting for either of them is a party, to the same extent as specified in the declaration.

Article 20

Uniform interpretation

In the interpretation of this Convention, regard shall be had to its international character and to the need to promote uniformity in its application.

Article 21

[Omitted]

Article 22

Non-unified legal systems

1. In relation to a Contracting State in which two or more systems of law apply in different territorial units with regard to any matter dealt with in this Convention –
   - (a) any reference to the law or procedure of a State shall be construed as referring, where appropriate, to the law or procedure in force in the relevant territorial unit;
   - (b) any reference to the court or courts of a State shall be construed as referring, where appropriate, to the court or courts in the relevant territorial unit;
   - (c) any reference to a connection with a State shall be construed as referring, where appropriate, to a connection with the relevant territorial unit;
   - (d) any reference to a connecting factor in relation to a State shall be construed as referring, where appropriate, to that connecting factor in relation to the relevant territorial unit.
2. Notwithstanding paragraph 1, a Contracting State with two or more territorial units in which different systems of law apply shall not be bound to apply this Convention to situations which involve solely such different territorial units.
3. A court in a territorial unit of a Contracting State with two or more territorial units in which different systems of law apply shall not be bound to recognise or enforce a judgment from another Contracting State solely because the judgment has been recognised or enforced in another territorial unit of the same Contracting State under this Convention.
4. This Article shall not apply to Regional Economic Integration Organisations.

Article 23

Relationship with other international instruments

1. This Convention shall be interpreted so far as possible to be compatible with other treaties in force for Contracting States, whether concluded before or after this Convention.
2. This Convention shall not affect the application by a Contracting State of a treaty that was concluded before this Convention.
3. This Convention shall not affect the application by a Contracting State of a treaty concluded after this Convention as concerns the recognition or enforcement of a judgment given by a court of a Contracting State that is also a Party to that treaty. Nothing in the other treaty shall affect the obligations under Article 6 towards Contracting States that are not Parties to that treaty.
4. This Convention shall not affect the application of the rules of a Regional Economic Integration Organisation that is a Party to this Convention as concerns the recognition or enforcement of a judgment given by a court of a Contracting State that is also a Member State of the Regional Economic Integration Organisation where –

   (a) the rules were adopted before this Convention was concluded; or
   (b) the rules were adopted after this Convention was concluded, to the extent that they do not affect the obligations under Article 6 towards Contracting States that are not Member States of the Regional Economic Integration Organisation.

Chapter IV – final clauses

Articles 24–32 [Omitted]

Section IV

Rules, Model Laws and Technical Notes

11 HCCH Principles on Choice of Law in International Commercial Contracts (Approved on 19 March 2015)

Preamble

This instrument sets forth general principles concerning choice of law in international commercial contracts. They affirm the principle of party autonomy with limited exceptions.

They may be used as a model for national, regional, supranational or international instruments.

They may be used to interpret, supplement and develop rules of private international law.

They may be applied by courts and by arbitral tribunals.

Article 1

Scope of the Principles

1. These Principles apply to choice of law in international contracts where each party is acting in the exercise of its trade or profession. They do not apply to consumer or employment contracts.
2. For the purposes of these Principles, a contract is international unless each party has its establishment in the same State and the relationship of the parties and all other relevant elements, regardless of the chosen law, are connected only with that State.
3. These Principles do not address the law governing –
   - (a) the capacity of natural persons;
   - (b) arbitration agreements and agreements on choice of court;
   - (c) companies or other collective bodies and trusts;
   - (d) insolvency;
   - (e) the proprietary effects of contracts;
   - (f) the issue of whether an agent is able to bind a principal to a third party.

DOI: 10.4324/9781003673194-15

Article 2

Freedom of choice

1. A contract is governed by the law chosen by the parties.
2. The parties may choose –

   (a) the law applicable to the whole contract or to only part of it; and
   (b) different laws for different parts of the contract.

3. The choice may be made or modified at any time. A choice or modification made after the contract has been concluded shall not prejudice its formal validity or the rights of third parties.
4. No connection is required between the law chosen and the parties or their transaction.

Article 3

Rules of law

The law chosen by the parties may be rules of law that are generally accepted on an international, supranational or regional level as a neutral and balanced set of rules, unless the law of the forum provides otherwise.

Article 4

Express and tacit choice

A choice of law, or any modification of a choice of law, must be made expressly or appear clearly from the provisions of the contract or the circumstances. An agreement between the parties to confer jurisdiction on a court or an arbitral tribunal to determine disputes under the contract is not in itself equivalent to a choice of law.

Article 5

Formal validity of the choice of law

A choice of law is not subject to any requirement as to form unless otherwise agreed by the parties.

Article 6

Agreement on the choice of law and battle of forms

1. Subject to paragraph 2 –

(a) whether the parties have agreed to a choice of law is determined by the law that was purportedly agreed to;
(b) if the parties have used standard terms designating two different laws and under both of these laws the same standard terms prevail, the law designated in the prevailing terms applies; if under these laws different standard terms prevail, or if under one or both of these laws no standard terms prevail, there is no choice of law.

2. The law of the State in which a party has its establishment determines whether that party has consented to the choice of law if, under the circumstances, it would not be reasonable to make that determination under the law specified in paragraph 1.

Article 7

Severability

A choice of law cannot be contested solely on the ground that the contract to which it applies is not valid.

Article 8

Exclusion of renvoi

A choice of law does not refer to rules of private international law of the law chosen by the parties unless the parties expressly provide otherwise.

Article 9

Scope of the chosen law

1. The law chosen by the parties shall govern all aspects of the contract between the parties, including but not limited to –

   (a) interpretation;
   (b) rights and obligations arising from the contract;
   (c) performance and the consequences of non-performance, including the assessment of damages;
   (d) the various ways of extinguishing obligations, and prescription and limitation periods;
   (e) validity and the consequences of invalidity of the contract;
   (f) burden of proof and legal presumptions;
   (g) pre-contractual obligations.

2. Paragraph 1(e) does not preclude the application of any other governing law supporting the formal validity of the contract.

Article 10

Assignment

In the case of contractual assignment of a creditor's rights against a debtor arising from a contract between the debtor and creditor –

(a) if the parties to the contract of assignment have chosen the law governing that contract, the law chosen governs mutual rights and obligations of the creditor and the assignee arising from their contract;
(b) if the parties to the contract between the debtor and creditor have chosen the law governing that contract, the law chosen governs –

   (i) whether the assignment can be invoked against the debtor;
   (ii) the rights of the assignee against the debtor; and
   (iii) whether the obligations of the debtor have been discharged.

Article 11

Overriding mandatory rules and public policy (ordre public)

1. These Principles shall not prevent a court from applying overriding mandatory provisions of the law of the forum which apply irrespective of the law chosen by the parties.
2. The law of the forum determines when a court may or must apply or take into account overriding mandatory provisions of another law.
3. A court may exclude application of a provision of the law chosen by the parties only if and to the extent that the result of such application would be manifestly incompatible with fundamental notions of public policy (ordre public) of the forum.
4. The law of the forum determines when a court may or must apply or take into account the public policy (ordre public) of a State the law of which would be applicable in the absence of a choice of law.
5. These Principles shall not prevent an arbitral tribunal from applying or taking into account public policy (ordre public), or from applying or taking into account overriding mandatory provisions of a law other than the law chosen by the parties, if the arbitral tribunal is required or entitled to do so.

Article 12

Establishment

If a party has more than one establishment, the relevant establishment for the purpose of these Principles is the one which has the closest relationship to the contract at the time of its conclusion.

12 UNCITRAL Mediation Rules 2021

Article 1. Application of the Rules

1. Where parties have agreed that disputes between them shall be submitted to mediation under the UNCITRAL Mediation Rules, then these Rules shall apply. The Rules may apply irrespective of the basis, whether contractual or not, upon which the mediation is carried out.
2. Mediation under the Rules is a process, whether referred to by the term mediation, conciliation or an expression of similar import, whereby parties request a third person or persons ("the mediator") to assist them in their attempt to reach an amicable settlement of their dispute. The mediator shall not have the authority to impose upon the parties a solution to the dispute.
3. The parties to a mediation shall be presumed to have referred to the Rules in effect on the date of commencement of the mediation, unless the parties have agreed to apply a particular version of the Rules.
4. The parties may agree to exclude or vary any provision of the Rules at any time.
5. Where any provision of these Rules is in conflict with a provision of the law applicable to the mediation from which the parties cannot derogate, including any applicable instrument or court order, that provision of law shall prevail.

Article 2. Commencement of mediation

1. Mediation in respect of a dispute that has arisen shall be deemed to have commenced on the day on which the parties to that dispute agree to engage in mediation, unless otherwise agreed.
2. If a party that invited another party to mediate does not receive an acceptance of the invitation within 30 days from the day on which the invitation was sent by any means that provides for a record of its transmission, or

DOI: 10.4324/9781003673194-16

within such other period of time as specified in the invitation, the party may elect to treat this as a rejection of the invitation to mediate.

Article 3. Number and appointment of mediators

1. There should be one mediator, unless otherwise agreed. Where there is more than one mediator, the mediators shall act jointly.
2. The parties should endeavour to appoint a mediator by agreement, unless a different appointment procedure applies. They may agree to replace a mediator at any time.
3. The parties may seek the assistance of an institution or person for appointing a mediator.
4. In recommending or selecting individuals to act as mediator, the institution or person shall have regard to:

   a. The professional expertise and qualifications of the prospective mediator, experience as a mediator and ability to conduct the mediation;
   b. Any relevant accreditation and/or certification awarded to the prospective mediator by a recognized professional mediation standards body;
   c. The availability of the mediator; and
   d. Such considerations as are likely to secure the appointment of an independent and impartial mediator.

5. If the parties have different nationalities, the institution or person, in consultation with the parties, may also take into account the advisability of appointing a mediator of a nationality other than the nationalities of the parties. In addition, the institution or person, in selecting, shall take into consideration geographical diversity and gender of the candidates.
6. When a person is approached in connection with a possible appointment as mediator, that person shall disclose any circumstances likely to give rise to justifiable doubts as to his or her impartiality or independence, including the disclosure of details of any personal, professional, financial or other interest that may influence the outcome of the dispute. A mediator, from the time of appointment and throughout the mediation, shall, without delay, disclose to the parties any such circumstances as they arise.
7. Prior to accepting the appointment, the prospective mediator shall ensure his or her availability to conduct the mediation diligently and efficiently.
8. In the event the mediator cannot perform her or his functions, the parties shall appoint a substitute mediator pursuant to the procedure mentioned in paragraphs 2, 3, 4, and 5. Paragraph 6 and 7 shall apply to the newly appointed mediator.

Article 4. Conduct of mediation

1. The parties may agree on the manner in which the mediation is to be conducted. Otherwise, the mediator may determine the conduct of the mediation in consultation with the parties, taking into account the circumstances of the case, any wishes that the parties may express and the need for a speedy settlement of the dispute.
2. The mediator shall maintain fair treatment of the parties and, in so doing, shall take into account the circumstances of the case.
3. In order to facilitate the conduct of the mediation:

    a. The parties and the mediator may convene a meeting at an early stage to agree on the organization of the mediation;
    b. The parties, or the mediator with the consent of the parties, may arrange for administrative assistance by a suitable institution or person; and
    c. The parties, or the mediator with the consent of the parties, may appoint experts.

4. In conducting the mediation, the mediator may, in consultation with the parties and taking into account the circumstances of the dispute, utilize any technological means as he or she considers appropriate, including to communicate with the parties and to hold meetings remotely.
5. A party may be represented or assisted by a person or persons of its choice. The name, address and function of such persons shall be communicated to all parties and to the mediator in advance of the mediation or without delay. This communication shall also indicate the scope of authority and whether the purpose of the appointment is for representation or assistance.

Article 5. Communication between the parties and the mediator

1. The mediator may meet or communicate with the parties together or with each of them separately.
2. At any stage of the mediation, the parties may submit information concerning the dispute, such as statements describing the general nature of the dispute, the points at issue, and any supporting document or additional information deemed appropriate. The information may also include a description of the goals, interests, needs and motivations of the parties as well as any relevant documents.
3. When the mediator receives information concerning the dispute from a party, the mediator shall keep such information confidential, unless that party indicates that the information is not subject to the condition that it

should be kept confidential, or expresses its consent to the disclosure of such information to another party to the mediation.

Article 6. Confidentiality

Unless otherwise agreed by the parties, all information relating to the mediation, including, if relevant, the settlement agreement, shall be kept confidential by those involved in the mediation, except where disclosure is required by the law or as referred to under article 8, paragraph 4.

Article 7. Introduction of evidence in other proceedings

1. Unless otherwise agreed by the parties, a party to the mediation, the mediator and any third person, including those involved in the administration of the mediation shall not, in arbitral, judicial or other dispute resolution proceedings, rely on, introduce as evidence or give evidence regarding any of the following:

    a. An invitation by a party to engage in mediation or the fact that a party was willing to participate in mediation;
    b. Views expressed, or suggestions made by a party in the mediation in respect of a possible settlement of the dispute;
    c. Statements or admissions made by a party in the course of the mediation;
    d. Proposals made by the mediator or the parties;
    e. The fact that a party had indicated its willingness to accept a proposal (or parts thereof) for settlement made by the mediator or the parties; and
    f. A document prepared primarily for purposes of the mediation.

2. Paragraph 1 applies irrespective of the form of the information or evidence referred to therein.
3. Paragraphs 1 and 2 apply whether or not the arbitral, judicial, or other dispute resolution proceedings relate to the dispute that is or was the subject matter of the mediation.
4. Subject to the limitations of paragraph 1, evidence that is otherwise admissible in arbitral, judicial, or other dispute resolution proceedings does not become inadmissible as a consequence of having been used or disclosed in the mediation.

Article 8. Settlement agreement

1. Once the parties agree on the terms of a settlement to resolve all or part of the dispute through mediation, they should prepare and sign a settlement

agreement. If requested by the parties and if the mediator deems it appropriate, the mediator may provide support to the parties in preparing the settlement agreement.

2. Unless otherwise agreed by the parties, the mediator or the mediation institution may sign or stamp the settlement agreement or provide other evidence that the agreement resulted from mediation.
3. The requirement that a settlement agreement shall be signed by the parties is met in relation to an electronic communication if:

   a. A method is used to identify the parties and to indicate the parties' intention in respect of the information contained in the electronic communication;
   b. The method is used either:

      (i) As reliable as appropriate for the purpose for which the electronic communication was generated or communicated, in the light of all the circumstances, including any relevant agreement; or
      (ii) Proven in fact to have fulfilled the functions described in subparagraph *(a)* above, by itself or together with further evidence.

4. By signing the settlement agreement, the parties agree that the settlement agreement can be used as evidence that it results from mediation, and that it can be relied upon for seeking relief under the applicable law.

Article 9. Termination of mediation

The mediation shall terminate:

a. By the signing of the settlement agreement by the parties, on the date of the agreement or such other date as agreed by the parties in the settlement agreement;
b. By a declaration of the parties to the mediator to the effect that the mediation is terminated, on the date of the declaration;
c. By a declaration of a party to the other party and the mediator, if appointed, to the effect that it no longer wishes to pursue mediation, on the date of the declaration;
d. By a declaration of the mediator, after consultation with the parties, to the effect that further efforts at mediation are no longer justified, on the date of the declaration;
e. By a declaration of the mediator, after consultation with the parties, in the situation referred to in article 11, paragraph 5, on the date of the declaration; or

f. At the expiration of any mandatory period in the applicable international instrument, court order or mandatory statutory provision, or as agreed upon by the parties.

Article 10. Arbitral, judicial, or other dispute resolution proceedings

1. Mediation may take place under the Rules at any time regardless of whether arbitral, judicial, or other dispute resolution proceedings have been already initiated.
2. Where the parties have agreed to mediate and have also expressly undertaken not to initiate, during a specified period of time or until a specified event has occurred, arbitral, judicial or other dispute resolution proceedings with respect to an existing or future dispute, such an undertaking shall be complied with, except to the extent necessary for a party, in its opinion, to preserve its rights. Initiation of such proceedings is not of itself to be regarded as waiver of the agreement to mediate or as a termination of the mediation.

Article 11. Costs and deposit of costs

1. The method for fixing the costs of mediation should be agreed upon by the parties and the mediator as early as possible in the mediation. Upon termination of the mediation, the mediator shall fix the costs of the mediation, which shall be reasonable in amount and give written notice thereof to the parties. The term "costs" includes only:

    a. The fees of the mediator;
    b. The travel and other expenses of the mediator;
    c. The cost of expert advice requested by the mediator with the agreement of the parties;
    d. The cost of any assistance provided pursuant to article 3, paragraph 3, and article 4, paragraph 3, of the Rules; and
    e. Any other expenses that may have been accrued out of the mediation, including in relation to translation and interpretation services.

2. Unless otherwise agreed by the parties, the costs, referred to in paragraph 1, are borne equally by the parties and, in the case of multiparty mediation, they are shared pro rata. All other expenses incurred by a party are borne by that party.
3. The mediator, upon appointment, may request each party to deposit an equal amount as an advance for the costs referred to in paragraph 1, unless otherwise agreed by the parties and the mediator.

4. During the course of the mediation, the mediator may request supplementary deposits in an equal amount from each party, unless otherwise agreed by the parties and the mediator.
5. If the required deposits under paragraphs 3 and 4 are not paid in full by all parties within a reasonable period set by the mediator, the mediator may suspend the mediation or may declare the termination of the mediation, in accordance with article 9, subparagraph (e).
6. Upon termination of the mediation and if deposits were received, the mediator shall render an accounting to the parties of the deposits received and return any unexpended funds to the parties.

Article 12. Role of the mediator in other proceedings

1. Unless otherwise agreed by the parties, the mediator shall not act as an arbitrator in respect of the dispute that was or is the subject of the mediation and of a dispute that has arisen from the same or a related contract or legal relationship.
2. The mediator shall not act as a representative or counsel of a party in any arbitral, judicial or other dispute resolution proceedings in respect of the dispute that was or is the subject of the mediation and of a dispute that has arisen from the same or a related contract or legal relationship.
3. The parties shall not present the mediator as a witness in any such proceedings.

Article 13. Exclusion of liability

Save for intentional wrongdoing, the parties waive, to the fullest extent permitted under the applicable law, any claim against the mediator based on any act or omission in connection with the mediation.

13 UNCITRAL Model Law on Electronic Transferable Records 2017

Chapter I: General Provisions

Article 1. Scope of application

1. This Law applies to electronic transferable records.
2. Other than as provided for in this Law, nothing in this Law affects the application to an electronic transferable record of any rule of law governing a transferable document or instrument including any rule of law applicable to consumer protection.
3. This Law does not apply to securities, such as shares and bonds, and other investment instruments, and to [...].[1]

Article 2. Definitions

For the purposes of this Law:

"Electronic record" means information generated, communicated, received or stored by electronic means, including, where appropriate, all information logically associated with or otherwise linked together so as to become part of the record, whether generated contemporaneously or not;

"Electronic transferable record" is an electronic record that complies with the requirements of article 10;

"Transferable document or instrument" means a document or instrument issued on paper that entitles the holder to claim the performance of the obligation indicated in the document or instrument and to transfer

1 The enacting jurisdiction may consider including a reference to: (a) documents and instruments that may be considered transferable, but that should not fall under the scope of the Model Law; (b) documents and instruments falling under the scope of the Convention Providing a Uniform Law for Bills of Exchange and Promissory Notes (Geneva, 1930) and the Convention Providing a Uniform Law for Cheques (Geneva, 1931); and (c) electronic transferable records existing only in electronic form.

DOI: 10.4324/9781003673194-17

the right to performance of the obligation indicated in the document or instrument through the transfer of that document or instrument.

Article 3. Interpretation

1. This Law is derived from a model law of international origin. In the interpre-tation of this Law, regard is to be had to the international origin and to the need to promote uniformity in its application.
2. Questions concerning matters governed by this Law which are not expressly settled in it are to be settled in conformity with the general principles on which this Law is based.

Article 4. Party autonomy and privity of contract

1. The parties may derogate from or vary by agreement the following provisions of this Law: [...].[2]
2. Such an agreement does not affect the rights of any person that is not a party to that agreement.

Article 5. Information requirements

Nothing in this Law affects the application of any rule of law that may require a person to disclose its identity, place of business or other information, or relieves a person from the legal consequences of making inaccurate, incomplete or false statements in that regard.

Article 6. Additional information in electronic transferable records

Nothing in this Law precludes the inclusion of information in an electronic transferable record in addition to that contained in a transferable document or instrument.

Article 7. Legal recognition of an electronic transferable record

1. An electronic transferable record shall not be denied legal effect, validity or enforceability on the sole ground that it is in electronic form.
2. Nothing in this Law requires a person to use an electronic transferable record without that person's consent.

2 The enacting jurisdiction may consider which provisions of the Model Law, if any, the parties may derogate from or vary by agreement.

3. The consent of a person to use an electronic transferable record may be inferred from the person's conduct.

Chapter II. Provisions on Functional Equivalence

Article 8. Writing

Where the law requires that information should be in writing, that requirement is met with respect to an electronic transferable record if the information contained therein is accessible so as to be usable for subsequent reference.

Article 9. Signature

Where the law requires or permits a signature of a person, that requirement is met by an electronic transferable record if a reliable method is used to identify that person and to indicate that person's intention in respect of the information contained in the electronic transferable record.

Article 10. Transferable documents or instruments

1. Where the law requires a transferable document or instrument, that requirement is met by an electronic record if:

   (a) The electronic record contains the information that would be required to be contained in a transferable document or instrument; and

   (b) A reliable method is used:

      (i) To identify that electronic record as the electronic transferable record;

      (ii) To render that electronic record capable of being subject to control from its creation until it ceases to have any effect or validity; and

      (iii) To retain the integrity of that electronic record.

2. The criterion for assessing integrity shall be whether information contained in the electronic transferable record, including any authorized change that arises from its creation until it ceases to have any effect or validity, has remained complete and unaltered apart from any change which arises in the normal course of communication, storage and display.

Article 11. Control

1. Where the law requires or permits the possession of a transferable document or instrument, that requirement is met with respect to an electronic transferable record if a reliable method is used:

(a) person; and
(b) To establish exclusive control of that electronic transferable record by a to identify that person as the person in control.

2. Where the law requires or permits transfer of possession of a transferable document or instrument, that requirement is met with respect to an electronic transferable record through the transfer of control over the electronic transferable record.

Chapter III. Use of Electronic Transferable Records

Article 12. General reliability standard

For the purposes of articles 9, 10, 11, 13, 16, 17 and 18, the method referred to shall be:

(a) As reliable as appropriate for the fulfilment of the function for which the method is being used, in the light of all relevant circumstances, which may include:

 (i) Any operational rules relevant to the assessment of reliability;
 (ii) The assurance of data integrity;
 (iii) The ability to prevent unauthorized access to and use of the system;
 (iv) The security of hardware and software;
 (v) The regularity and extent of audit by an independent body;
 (vi) The existence of a declaration by a supervisory body, an accreditation body or a voluntary scheme regarding the reliability of the method;
 (vii) Any applicable industry standard; or

(b) Proven in fact to have fulfilled the function by itself or together with further evidence.

Article 13. Indication of time and place in electronic transferable records

Where the law requires or permits the indication of time or place with respect to a transferable document or instrument, that requirement is met if a reliable method is used to indicate that time or place with respect to an electronic transferable record.

Article 14. Place of business

1. A location is not a place of business merely because that is:

   (a) Where equipment and technology supporting an information system used by a party in connection with electronic transferable records are located; or

   (b) Where the information system may be accessed by other parties.

2. The sole fact that a party makes use of an electronic address or other element of an information system connected to a specific country does not create a presumption that its place of business is located in that country.

Article 15. Endorsement

Where the law requires or permits the endorsement in any form of a transferable document or instrument, that requirement is met with respect to an electronic transferable record if the information required for the endorsement is included in the electronic transferable record and that information is compliant with the requirements set forth in articles 8 and 9.

Article 16. Amendment

Where the law requires or permits the amendment of a transferable document or instrument, that requirement is met with respect to an electronic transferable record if a reliable method is used for amendment of information in the electronic transferable record so that the amended information is identified as such.

Article 17. Replacement of a transferable document or instrument with an electronic transferable record

1. An electronic transferable record may replace a transferable document or instrument if a reliable method for the change of medium is used.
2. For the change of medium to take effect, a statement indicating a change of medium shall be inserted in the electronic transferable record.
3. Upon issuance of the electronic transferable record in accordance with para-graphs 1 and 2, the transferable document or instrument shall be made inoperative and ceases to have any effect or validity.
4. A change of medium in accordance with paragraphs 1 and 2 shall not affect the rights and obligations of the parties.

Article 18. Replacement of an electronic transferable record with a transferable document or instrument

1. A transferable document or instrument may replace an electronic transferable record if a reliable method for the change of medium is used.
2. For the change of medium to take effect, a statement indicating a change of medium shall be inserted in the transferable document or instrument.
3. Upon issuance of the transferable document or instrument in accordance with paragraphs 1 and 2, the electronic transferable record shall be made inoperative and ceases to have any effect or validity.
4. A change of medium in accordance with paragraphs 1 and 2 shall not affect the rights and obligations of the parties.

Chapter IV. Cross-Border Recognition of Electronic Transferable Records

Article 19. Non-discrimination of foreign electronic transferable records

1. An electronic transferable record shall not be denied legal effect, validity or enforceability on the sole ground that it was issued or used abroad.
2. Nothing in this Law affects the application to electronic transferable records of rules of private international law governing a transferable document or instrument.

14 UNCITRAL Model Law on Automated Contracting 2024

Article 1. Definitions

1. For the purposes of this Law:

   (a) "Automated system" means a computer system that is capable of carrying out actions without the necessary review or intervention of a natural person;
   (b) "Data message" means information generated, sent, received or stored by electronic, magnetic, optical or similar means.

2. An automated system may be programmed to operate in a deterministic or non-deterministic manner.

Article 2. Scope of application

1. This Law applies to the use of automated systems to form or to perform con-tracts, including by:

   (a) Generating or otherwise processing data messages that constitute an action in connection with the formation of contracts, such as an offer or acceptance of an offer;
   (b) Generating or otherwise processing data messages that constitute an action in connection with the performance of a contract, such as its modification or termination.

2. Nothing in this Law affects the application of any rule of law that may govern the design, commissioning, operation or use of automated systems.

Article 3. Interpretation

1. In the interpretation of this Law, regard is to be had to its international origin and to the need to promote uniformity in its application and the observance of good faith.

DOI: 10.4324/9781003673194-18

2. Questions concerning matters governed by this Law which are not expressly settled in it are to be settled in conformity with the general principles on which this Law is based.

Article 4. Technology neutrality

Nothing in this Law requires the use of an automated system or a particular method in automated systems to form or perform contracts.

Article 5. Legal recognition of automated contracting

1. A contract formed using an automated system shall not be denied validity or enforceability on the sole ground that no natural person reviewed or intervened in any action carried out in connection with the formation of the contract.
2. A contract performed using an automated system shall not be denied validity or enforceability on the sole ground that no natural person reviewed or intervened in any action carried out in connection with the performance of the contract.][1]
3. An action carried out by an automated system in connection with the formation or performance of a contract shall not be denied legal effect, validity or enforceability on the sole ground that no natural person reviewed or intervened in the action.

Article 6. Legal recognition of contracts in computer code and use of dynamic information in automated contracting

1. A contract shall not be denied validity or enforceability on the sole ground that the terms of the contract are contained in data messages in the form of computer code.
2. A contract shall not be denied validity or enforceability on the sole ground that the terms of the contract incorporate information from a data source that provides information that changes periodically or continuously.
3. An action in connection with the formation of a contract shall not be denied legal effect, validity or enforceability on the sole ground that the action involves processing data messages containing information from a source that provides information that changes periodically or continuously.

1 States that wish to extend the scope of article 5 to cover contracts that are performed using an automated system may wish to enact this provision.

Article 7. Attribution of actions carried out by automated systems

1. As between the parties to a contract, an action carried out by an automated system is attributed in accordance with a procedure agreed to by the parties.
2. If paragraph 1 does not apply, an action carried out by an automated system is attributed to the person who uses the system for that purpose.
3. Attribution of an action carried out by an automated system shall not be denied on the sole ground that the outcome was unexpected.
4. Nothing in this article affects the application of any rule of law that may govern the legal consequences of attributing an action carried out by an automated system to a person.

[Article 8. Unexpected actions carried out by automated systems

1. Unless otherwise agreed by the parties, where an action carried out by an automated system is attributed to a party to a contract, the other party to the contract is not entitled to rely on that action if, in the light of all the circumstances:

   (a) The party to which the action is attributed could not reasonably have expected the action; and
   (b) The other party knew or could reasonably be expected to have known that the party to which the action is attributed did not expect the action.

2. Nothing in this article affects the application of any rule of law or agreement of the parties that may govern the legal consequences of an action carried out by an automated system.][2]

Article 9. Information requirements

Nothing in this Law affects the application of any rule of law that may require a person to disclose information on the design, operation or use of an

2 This provision is included for States wishing to enact one or more specific provisions addressing unexpected actions carried out by automated systems.

automated system, or provides legal consequences for failing to do so or for disclosing inaccurate, incomplete or false information.

Article 10. Non-avoidance

Unless otherwise provided by law, a party shall not be relieved from the legal consequences of its failure to comply with a rule of law on the sole ground that it used an automated system.

15 UNCITRAL Technical Notes on Online Dispute Resolution

Section I — Introduction

Overview of online dispute resolution

1. In tandem with the sharp increase of online cross-border transactions, there has been a need for mechanisms for resolving disputes which arise from such transactions.
2. One such mechanism is online dispute resolution ("ODR"), which can assist the parties in resolving the dispute in a simple, fast, flexible and secure manner, without the need for physical presence at a meeting or hearing. ODR encompasses a broad range of approaches and forms (including but not limited to ombudsmen, complaints boards, negotiation, conciliation, mediation, facilitated settlement, arbitration and others),[1] and the potential for hybrid processes comprising both online and offline elements. As such, ODR represents significant opportunities for access to dispute resolution by buyers and sellers concluding cross-border commercial transactions, both in developed and developing countries.

Purpose of the Technical Notes

3. The purpose of the Technical Notes is to foster the development of ODR and to assist ODR administrators, ODR platforms, neutrals, and the parties to ODR proceedings.

1 The order of the list of approaches or forms in brackets is presented in increasing order of formality, reflecting the approach taken in the description of commonly-used methods for settling disputes contained in UNCITRAL's Legislative Guide on Privately Financed Infrastructure Projects (2000), available at www.uncitral.org/uncitral/uncitral_texts/procurement_infrastructure.html. Furthermore, the terms are illustrative only, relative formality may vary from system to system, and relevant processes in some jurisdictions may be known by more than one of the terms contained in the list itself.

DOI: 10.4324/9781003673194-19

4. The Technical Notes reflect approaches to ODR systems that embody principles of impartiality, independence, efficiency, effectiveness, due process, fairness, accountability and transparency.
5. The Technical Notes are intended for use in disputes arising fromcross-border low-value sales or service contracts concluded using electronic communications. They do not promote any practice of ODR as best practice.

Non-binding nature of the Technical Notes

6. The Technical Notes are a descriptive document. They are not intended to be exhaustive or exclusive, nor are they suitable to be used as rules for any ODR proceeding. They do not impose any legal requirement binding on the parties or any persons and/or entities administering or enabling an ODR proceeding, and do not imply any modification to any ODR rules that the parties may have selected.

Section II — Principles

7. The principles that underpin any ODR process include fairness, transparency, due process and accountability.
8. ODR may assist in addressing a situation arising out of cross-border e-commerce transactions, namely the fact that traditional judicial mechanisms for legal recourse may not offer an adequate solution for cross-border e-commerce disputes.
9. ODR ought to be simple, fast and efficient, in order to be able to be used in a "real world setting", including that it should not impose costs, delays and burdens that are disproportionate to the economic value at stake.

Transparency

10. It is desirable to disclose any relationship between the ODR administrator and a particular vendor, so that users of the service are informed of potential conflicts of interest.
11. The ODR administrator may wish to publish anonymized data or statistics on outcomes in ODR processes, in order to enable parties to assess its overall record, consistent with applicable principles of confidentiality.
12. All relevant information should be available on the ODR administrator's website in a user-friendly and accessible manner.

Independence

13. It is desirable for the ODR administrator to adopt a code of ethics for its neutrals, in order to guide neutrals as to conflicts of interest and other rules of conduct.

14. It is useful for the ODR administrator to adopt policies dealing with identifying and handling conflicts of interest.

Expertise

15. The ODR administrator may wish to implement comprehensive policies governing selection and training of neutrals.
16. An internal oversight/quality assurance process may help the ODR administrator to ensure that a neutral conforms with the standards it has set for itself.

Consent

17. The ODR process should be based on the explicit and informed consent of the parties.

Section III — Stages of an ODR proceeding

18. The process of an ODR proceeding may consist of stages including: negotiation; facilitated settlement; and a third (final) stage.
19. When a claimant submits a notice through the ODR platform to the ODR administrator (see section VI below), the ODR administrator informs the respondent of the existence of the claim and the claimant of the response. The first stage of proceedings — a technology-enabled negotiation — commences, in which the claimant and respondent negotiate directly with one another through the ODR platform.
20. If that negotiation process fails (i.e. does not result in a settlement of the claim), the process may move to a second, "facilitated settlement stage (see paras 40 – 44 below)/ In that stage of ODR proceedings, the ODR administrator appoints a neutral (see para. 25 below),who communicates with the parties in an attempt to reach a settlement.
21. If facilitated settlement fails, a third and final stage of ODR proceedings may commence, in which case the ODR administrator or neutral may inform the parties of the nature of such stage.

Section IV — Scope of ODR process

22. An ODR process may be particularly useful for disputes arising out of cross-border, low-value e-commerce transactions. An ODR process may apply to disputes arising out of both a business-to-business as well as business-to-consumer transactions.

23. An ODR process may apply to disputes arising out of both sales and service contracts.

Section V — ODR definitions, roles and responsibilities, and communications

24. Online dispute resolution, or "ODR", is a "mechanism for resolving disputes through the use of electronic communications and other information and communication technology". The process may be implemented differently by different administrators of the process, and may evolve over time.
25. As used herein a "claimant" is the party initiating ODR proceedings and the "respondent" the party to whom the claimant's notice is directed, in line with traditional, offline, alternative dispute resolution nomenclature. A neutral is an individual that assists the parties in settling or resolving the dispute.
26. ODR requires a technology-based intermediary. In other words, unlike offline alternative dispute resolution, an ODR proceeding cannot be conducted on an ad hoc basis involving only the parties to a dispute and a neutral (that is, without an administrator). Instead, to permit the use of technology to enable a dispute resolution process, an ODR process requires a system for generating, sending, receiving, storing, exchanging or otherwise processing communications in a manner that ensures data security. Such a system is referred to herein as an "ODR platform".
27. An ODR platform should be administered and coordinated. The entity that carries out such administration and coordination is referred to herein as the "ODR administrator". The ODR administrator may be separate from or part of the ODR platform.
28. In order to enable ODR communications, it is desirable that both the ODR administrator and the ODR platform be specified in the dispute resolution clause.
29. The communications that may take place during the course of proceedings have been defined as "any communication (including a statement, declaration, demand, notice, response, submission, notification or request) made by means of information generated, sent, received or stored by electronic, magnetic, optical or similar means."
30. It is desirable that all communications in ODR proceedings take place via the ODR platform. Consequently, both the parties to the dispute, and the ODR platform itself, should have a designated "electronic address". The term "electronic address" is defined in other UNCITRAL texts.
31. To enhance efficiency it is desirable that the ODR administrator promptly

(a) Acknowledge receipt of any communication by the ODR platform;
(b) Notify parties of the availability of any communication received by the ODR platform; and
(c) Keep the parties informed of the commencement and conclusion of different stages of the proceedings.

32. In order to avoid loss of time, it is desirable that a communication be deemed to be received by a party when the administrator notifies that party of its availability on the platform; deadlines in the proceedings would run from the time the administrator has made that notification. At the same time, it is desirable that the ODR administrator be empowered to extend deadlines, in order to allow for some flexibility when appropriate.

Section VI — Commencement of ODR proceedings

33. In order that an ODR proceeding may begin, it is desirable that the claimant provide to the ODR administrator a notice containing the following information:

(a) The name and electronic address of the claimant and of the claimant's representative (if any) authorized to act for the claimant in the ODR proceedings;
(b) The name and electronic address of the respondent and of the respondent's representative (if any) known to the claimant;
(c) The grounds on which the claim is made;
(d) Any solutions proposed to resolve the dispute;
(e) The claimant's preferred language of proceedings; and
(f) The signature or other means of identification and authentication of the claimant and/or the claimant's representative.

34. ODR proceedings may be deemed to have commenced when, following a claimant's communication of a notice to the ODR administrator, the ODR administrator notifies the parties that the notice is available at the ODR platform.

35. It is desirable that the respondent communicate its response to the ODR administrator within a reasonable time of being notified of the availability of the claimant's notice on the ODR platform, and that the response include the following elements:

(a) The name and electronic address of the respondent and the respondent's representative (if any) authorized to act for the respondent in the ODR proceedings;
(b) A response to the grounds on which the claim is made;

(c) Any solutions proposed to resolve the dispute;
(d) The signature or other means of identification and authentication of the respondent and/or the respondent's representative; and
(e) Notice of any counterclaim containing the grounds on which the counterclaim is made.

36. As much as is possible, it is desirable that both the notice and response be accompanied by all documents and other evidence relied upon by each party, or contain references to them. In addition, to the extent that a claimant is pursuing any other legal remedies, it is desirable that such information also be provided with the notice.

Section VII — Negotiation

37. The first stage may be a negotiation, conducted between the parties via the ODR platform.
38. The first stage of proceedings may commence following the communication of the respondent's response to the ODR platform and:

    (a) Notification thereof to the claimant; or
    (b) Failing a response, the lapse of a reasonable period of time after the notice has been communicated to the respondent.

39. It is desirable that, if the negotiation does not result in a settlement within a reasonable period of time, the process proceed to the next stage.

Section VIII — Facilitated settlement

40. The second stage of ODR proceedings may be facilitated settlement, whereby a neutral is appointed and communicates with the parties to try to achieve a settlement.
41. That stage may commence if negotiation via the platform fails for any reason (including non-participation or failure to reach a settlement within a reasonable period of time), or where one or both parties to the dispute request to move directly to the next stage of proceedings.
42. Upon commencement of the facilitated settlement stage of proceedings, it is desirable that the ODR administrator appoint a neutral, and notify the parties of that appointment, and provide certain details about the identity of the neutral as described in paragraph 46 below.
43. In the facilitated settlement stage, it is desirable that the neutral communicate with the parties to try to achieve a settlement.
44. If a facilitated settlement cannot be achieved within a reasonable period of time, the process may move to a final stage.

Section IX — Final stage

45. If the neutral has not succeeded in facilitating the settlement, it is desirable that the ODR administrator or neutral informs the parties of the nature of the final stage, and of the form that it might take.

Section X — Appointment, powers and functions of the neutral

46. To enhance efficiency and reduce costs, it is preferable that the ODR administrator appoint a neutral only when a neutral is required for a dispute resolution process in accordance with any applicable ODR rules. At the point in an ODR proceeding at which a neutral is required for the dispute resolution process, it is desirable that the ODR administrator "promptly" appoint the neutral (i.e., generally at the commencement of the facilitated settlement stage of proceedings). Upon appointment, it is desirable that the ODR administrator promptly notify the parties of the name of the neutral and any other relevant or identifying information in relation to that neutral.
47. It is desirable that neutrals have the relevant professional experience as well as dispute resolution skills to enable them to deal with the dispute in question. However, subject to any professional regulation, ODR neutrals need not necessarily be qualified lawyers.
48. With regard to the appointment and functions of neutrals, it is desirable that:

    (a) The neutral's acceptance of his or her appointment operates to confirm that he or she has the time necessary to devote to the process;
    (b) The neutral be required to declare his or her impartiality and independence and disclose at any time any facts or circumstances that might give rise to likely doubts as to his or her impartiality or independence;
    (c) The ODR system provides parties with a method for objecting to the appointment of a neutral;
    (d) In the event of an objection to an appointment of a neutral,the ODR administrator be required to make a determination as to whether the neutral shall be replaced;
    (e) There be only one neutral per dispute appointed at any time for reasons of cost efficiency;
    (f) A party be entitled to object to the neutral receiving information generated during the negotiation period; and
    (g) If the neutral resigns or has to be replaced during the course of the ODR proceedings, the ODR administrator be required to appoint a replacement, subject to the same safeguards as set out during the appointment of the initial neutral.

49. In respect of the powers of the neutral, it is desirable that:

    (a) Subject to any applicable ODR rules, the neutral be enabled to conduct the ODR proceedings in such a manner as he or she considers appropriate;
    (b) The neutral be required to avoid unnecessary delay or expense in the conduct of the proceedings;
    (c) The neutral be required to provide a fair and efficient process for resolving disputes;
    (d) The neutral be required to remain independent, impartial and treat both parties equally throughout the proceedings;
    (e) The neutral be required to conduct proceedings based on such communications as are before the neutral during the proceedings;
    (f) The neutral be enabled to allow the parties to provide additional information in relation to the proceedings; and
    (g) The neutral be enabled to extend any deadlines set out in any applicable ODR rules for a reasonable time.

50. While the process for appointment of a neutral for an ODR proceeding is subject to the same due process standards that apply to that process in an offline context, it may be desirable to use streamlined appointment and challenge procedures in order to address the need for ODR to provide a simple, time-, and cost-effective alternative to traditional approaches to dispute resolution.

Section XI — Language

51. Technology tools available in ODR can offer a great deal of flexibility regarding the language used for the proceeding. Even where an ODR agreement or ODR rules specify a language to be used in proceedings, it is desirable that a party to the proceedings be able to indicate in the notice or response whether it wishes to proceed in a different language, so that the ODR administrator can identify other language options that the parties may select.

Section XII — Governance

52. It is desirable for guidelines (and/or minimum requirements) to exist in relation to the conduct of ODR platforms and administrators.
53. It is desirable that ODR proceedings be subject to the same confidentiality and due process standards that apply to dispute resolution proceedings in an offline context, in particular independence, neutrality and impartiality.

Made in the USA
Las Vegas, NV
19 September 2026

332f41c5-bb99-4118-aba7-dd7e2102d3dbR01